Biblical Code Found on the Face of the Great Pyramid Reveals

Biblical Code Found on the Face of the Great Pyramid Reveals

The Return of Christ In 2040

Gary Brannock

To order additional copies of this book, contact:
Xlibris Corporation
1-888-795-4274
www.Xlibris.com
Orders@Xlibris.com
109442

Contents

Introduction 7

Chapter 1   The Great Pyramid and the Ark Connection 9
Chapter 2   The Coffer . . . The Ark . . . The Object.........................15
Chapter 3   A Lighthouse to the Stars.................................18
Chapter 4   The Bible and the Pyramid Connection.........................21
Chapter 5   The Number 153.................................26
Chapter 6   The Missing Number.................................29
Chapter 7   Assembling the Calendar.................................35
Chapter 8   A Very Perplexing Clue 40
Chapter 9   The Dream 43
Chapter 10   "Seek and Ye Shall Find" 49
Chapter 11   The Number and the Calendar Revealed.........................53
Chapter 12   73 and 37 . . . What a Pair! 58
Chapter 13   They Have Eyes Yet Still do not See.........................62
Chapter 14   Hell and the Bottomless Pit 65
Chapter 15   Black Holes In Space.................................69
Chapter 16   Exposing the Miracles of the Beast.........................74
Chapter 17   Exposing the Image of the Beast.........................78
Chapter 18   The Rise and Fall of the Fourth Kingdom.........................81
Chapter 19   The New Tower of Babel?.................................89
Chapter 20   Coincidences to Huge too Ignore 94
Chapter 21   An Unheeded Warning Becomes Destiny 98

Summation 103

Introduction

It was a picture in either my fourth or fifth grade history book that first got my attention of the pyramids of Egypt. And just like many others before me, I was immediately fascinated at the sight of those uniquely designed and massive-sized stone formations. And since I attended church most every Sunday, I was also aware that they were situated in the same area as the Biblical Exodus. So from that moment forward, whenever I heard the story of Moses leading God's chosen people out of bondage, in my mind, I would always envision the Israelites walking right past those pyramids as they departed Egypt. But at the same time, I had also assumed it was just a mere coincidence that those pyramids happen to be located in the same place as the Exodus. After all, my history book had offered what seemed to be a perfectly logical explanation for their existence, which was that they were the burial tombs for Egypt's most-celebrated pharaohs. Therefore, it never occurred to me that the historians might be in error, and that the true purpose of why those monuments were built, has to this very day, remained one of the world's greatest unsolved mysteries.

My previous book began at Mount Sinai in an attempt to find out the truth about what happened to the lost Ark of the Covenant by tracing its possible path throughout history. But as that book came to its conclusion, I was told that I must once again return to Sinai for there was more that was yet to be revealed. And since I had moved forward in time in my quest for the Ark, I instinctively knew that this search was going to take me into the past, back to ancient Egypt, to Exodus, and to the pyramids.

Therefore, this book begins by comparing the Ark of the Covenant to the stone coffer inside of the Great Pyramid of Giza. Is it possible there was at one time a mysterious and powerful object housed inside of the Great Pyramid? And could it have been removed at the same moment of the Exodus and then later placed in the Ark giving it its mystical other worldly powers? When I begin attempting to answer these questions, the Exodus takes on a whole new perspective exposing many revelations, which eventually sheds a huge new light on this Biblical event.

But that's not all, for I also found something within the Great Pyramid of monumental significance, and even though I didn't know what it meant, I still knew it was of great importance because it was directly related to Jesus Christ. Thus, I began a quest in a determined obsession to dissect and unlock its secrets. And when I finally begin to succeed and start unraveling its mysteries, it reveals connections of the Great Pyramid to God, Christ, and the Holy Bible in ways I could never have dreamed possible. As a result, the same thing that happened in my previous writing happens once again in which the more I search the Biblical past the more I am shown the Biblical future.

Please remember that in doing what I was told by returning to Mount Sinai, that this book is a chronological documentation of all that was found as I went where I was being led. Therefore, all that is revealed within these pages are in the order of which they were discovered.

Chapter 1

The Great Pyramid and the Ark Connection

The Bible's book of Exodus states once Moses had led God's chosen people out of Egypt they entered into a covenant with Him at Mount Sinai. It's there that the Ark of the Covenant was constructed by the Israelites with specific instructions from God. It's always been believed that the Ten Commandments, and possibly the spear of Aaron, were all that was placed inside of the Ark. But Exodus also states that when Moses sat upon the mercy seat, he could literally hear the voice of God. And knowing that the Ark could perform this amazing feat causes one to wonder as to whether there wasn't something else placed inside of the Ark along with those laws from God.

Within His special instructions on how it was to be built, God also gave precise measurements for the size of the Ark, which happened to be several times larger than needed to carry those stone tablets. So, why would God have the Israelites build an Ark much bigger than necessary to house those Commandments? This is where it begins to get interesting, because it's been the speculation among many scholars that those dimensions for the Ark are a very close match to the dimensions of the empty coffer found inside the Great Pyramid of Giza.

For centuries, it has been the popular and accepted belief that the Egyptian pyramids were used as burial tombs for Egypt's most highly worshipped pharaohs. Even the two main rooms inside of the Great Pyramid are referred to as the king and queens chambers. But there has never been as much as a single mummy found inside of any of the pyramids in Egypt, and this raises serious doubt that they were built to be used as the final resting place for any of Egypt's dead kings. And if they were not used as burial tombs, then the true purpose for the Egyptians building those huge complex structures has yet to be answered.

It's believed the Great Pyramid of Giza was completed around 2,600 BC. Observance of its huge stones makes it clear that it was built to be a marker that would withstand the test of time by enduring against any and all forces of nature. Computer calculations estimate there were around six hundred thousand blocks used in its construction. On average, these blocks weighed between two to three tons, yet some weighed as much as seventy tons. Its outer mantle comprised of 144,000 casing stones, which were highly polished and flat to an accuracy of 1/100 of an inch. Each one of these stones were about one hundred inches thick, weighing fifteen tons with nearly perfect right angles for all six of its sides. The sunlight reflecting from these polished stones could be seen from the mountains of Israel, and it's estimated that they were also visible from as far away as the moon.

When the height of the Great Pyramid is taken as the radius of a circle, then the circumference of this circle is the same as the perimeter of the base of the pyramid. This is known as the complimentary squaring of a circle and circling of a square. The base of the pyramid covers thirteen and six-tenths acres with each side greater than five acres in area and level to within one inch of perfection. The Great Pyramid is also located at the center of the land mass of the earth, and because of this and the way it was constructed, during the spring equinox, it does not cast a shadow. It also faces true north with only a 3/60th of a degree of error, which makes it the most accurately aligned structure on the planet.

The position of Egypt's three main pyramids on the ground represent a mirror reflection of the Orion constellation at its position in the sky dating back to at least 10,400 BC. The word pyramid is composed of the Greek words "pyra" meaning fire, visible, or light, and the word "midos" meaning measures, or, *visible light measures.*

The main entrance to the Great Pyramid is located on its north side seventeen steps up from its base and consists of two main passages. The entrance and the two main passages are twenty-four feet east of the center of the pyramid and the passages run north and south.

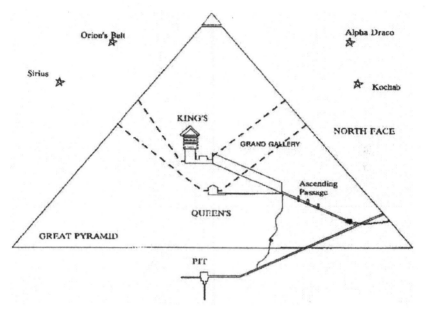

(The above design courtesy of Tim Hunkler)

The main entrance leads you down the first passage that continues for a total length of three hundred and forty feet. Yet at ninety-seven feet down the descending passage connects to the ascending passage, which continues upward for one hundred and twenty-four feet where it opens up to a wider passage known as the grand galley. It's here that you have one of two choices; you can continue through a horizontal passage for one hundred and twenty-seven feet, which will take you to what is known as the queen's chamber, or you can continue upward through the grand galley until you reach the room referred to as the king's chamber.

(The grand galley)

The grand galley is one hundred and fifty-three feet long and seven feet wide at its beginning. Its walls rise in seven courses of polished limestone, each corbelled three inches to the center. This makes the galley become narrower as you ascend it from sixty-one inches across at the bottom to forty-one inches at the top. On each side of the grand galley's floor leading up to the king's chamber is a ramp that is eighteen inches wide with slots at regular intervals.

Upon reaching the top of the grand galley, there is a narrow passage way that leads to an antechamber and its walls are no longer limestone but, instead, are red granite. On the other side of this chamber is the so-called king's chamber. Its walls are also made of granite and measures thirty-four feet by seventeen feet and is nineteen feet in height. Above the roof of the king's chamber is a series of five cavities. These were once thought to be there to relieve the pressure of the weight from above but recently that has come into question, so it's not clear as to their true purpose.

(The stone coffer in the king's chamber)

Located on the west side of the king's chamber is a stone coffer which is the only thing that has ever been found inside of the Great Pyramid. It has long thought to have been the empty sarcophagus of the Pharaoh Khufu. It measures six feet six inches long, two feet three inches wide, and three feet in depth. It has a huge chip on one top corner, and although it's never been found, it's believed at some point it had a lid because of a ridge that runs along its top edge. It's also assumed because of the narrow passage at the beginning of the antechamber that the coffer was placed in the king's chamber prior to the finishing of the passage way.

This thorough inspection of the Great Pyramid leaves one to concede that this structure could not have been built by an ancient civilization dating back a minimum of five thousand years unless they had received major input from a higher intelligence from an other worldly source. And since the Great Pyramid was not used as a burial chamber, then the true reason for its construction and its purpose for housing that stone coffer still remains a mystery.

So could it be that one of the reasons for the construction of the Great Pyramid was to house a mysterious and powerful other worldly object which was kept in that stone coffer? And could it also be that it was removed at the moment of the biblical Exodus, and then later at

Mount Sinai placed in the Ark of the Covenant? And moreover, could the key to solving the mystery of the Great Pyramid lie within gaining a better understanding of what was kept in that stone coffer by comparing it to the mysterious powers of the Ark?

Chapter 2

The Coffer . . . The Ark . . . The Object

A comparison of the coffer to the Ark for similarities may reveal a connection of them to the object. But even more important, this comparison may also reveal clues about the object's function before it was taken from the Great Pyramid.

Upon his return with the Ten Commandments from atop Mount Sinai, the Bible states that Moses had such an eerie glow about him that the Israelites were afraid of him. Soon after this incident they were instructed by God to build the Ark of the Covenant. Scripture states that it was made from a rare wood known as shittim, which was very hard and durable, similar to the bones of a human being. The Ark was then encased with gold inside and out; and on top of that gold plating was another layer of tach-hash which was thought to be the skin of an unknown animal that became extinct soon after the Ark's construction. And this leads one to ask; since the gold was covered by the skin of an animal then it was hidden from view; therefore, its purpose could not have been to show that God was wealthy in a worldly sense. So, could it be that the tach-hash and gold were used as insulators to contain a mysterious and powerful source of energy that was harmful to humans? After all, the book of Exodus states that only certain anointed ones could carry the Ark while all others who got close to it ran the risk of great bodily harm including death. And the mystery surrounding the Ark only deepens when taking its mystical powers into account. Scripture also states that it was the Ark that enabled the Israelites with the ability to defeat all their enemies, and when Moses sat upon the mercy seat, he could literally hear the voice of God.

The coffer inside the Great Pyramid was sawed out of a block of solid red granite which required bronze saws eight to nine feet long using teeth set with sapphires. Microscopic analysis revealed it was then hollowed out with a fixed point drill that used hard jeweled bits with a drilling force of two tons.

These comparisons instantly reveal the possibility of three major connections of the coffer and the Ark to the object. First, both the coffer and the Ark contained an object so powerful that it had to be housed in a thickly layered insulated container. Second, the Ark and the coffer, although not exact, were similar in size. Third, if an object was kept in the stone coffer of the Great Pyramid, then it could be said that it was removed at the same time in which Moses led the Israelites away from Egypt then later placed in the Ark of the Covenant at Mount Sinai.

The interior dimensions of the coffer are six feet six inches long, two feet three inches wide, and three feet in depth. The Ark was five feet two inches long, three feet one inch wide, and three feet one inch in depth. Since the Ark's dimensions were somewhat different from that of the coffer then it's possible that when the object was taken from the coffer, it was either reshaped or a portion of it was removed before it was placed inside of the Ark. Either way, this reveals that the object likely consisted of several interchangeable parts which could be retooled to change its shape and size.

When comparing the coffer and its ability to contain an object that emitted a powerful source of energy to that of the Ark then the reshaping or resizing of the object to lower its level of force; and or, more evenly distribute its weight makes perfect sense. The stone coffer was hollowed out from a block of solid red granite and the coffer itself was housed inside of the Great Pyramid. This gives an idea about just how powerful the force may have been that emanated from the object when it was in its entirety. But on the other hand, the Ark was made from wood, layered in gold and covered with the skin of an unknown animal. The coffer in the Great Pyramid was stationary. The Ark had to be carried through the desert to the promised land and again whenever the Israelites went to war. This makes it likely that the object was reshaped, and or, reduced in size to evenly distribute its weight to make it easier to carry, and also to reduce the intensity of its force so it could be kept in the less dense, less insulated Ark.

The question of how the Ark ensured the Israelites victory over their enemies has never been answered. But when researching the Bible for a clue, one finds the story of the walls of Jericho. The Israelites were instructed by God to carry the Ark and march around the walls once a day for seven days. Then on the seventh day when they blew their trumpets and shouted, the walls of Jericho collapsed. So could it be that the Ark interacted with the sound of those trumpets by amplifying that sound to a certain decibel which in turn caused those walls to fall? And was this how they defeated all their adversaries? When they carried the Ark with them into battle did they blow their trumpets knowing that the Ark would interact with that sound and render their foes helpless? While there is no way of knowing whether or not this actually happened, it is plausible; therefore, it must be considered that the object may have had the capability to interact with and affect sound waves.

With this new information it's now safe to assume the object may have had the following capabilities: 1. It consisted of a force so strong and dangerous that it had to be housed in a well-insulated container to control its deadly power. 2. It emanated a powerful source of light. 3. It may have consisted of several interchangeable and, or removable parts. 4. It may have had the ability to interact with and affect sound waves. 5. Upon the object being placed inside the Ark, it gave Moses the ability to hear the voice of God. And all these clues leaves one to wonder, just what could've been the object's function when it was housed in that stone coffer of the Great Pyramid?

Chapter 3

A Lighthouse to the Stars

It's the accepted belief among many mainstream scholars that etchings found on the wall of the descending passage of the Great Pyramid mark the date of its completion at 2,600 BC. Yet there are others who say the pyramids could be at least twelve thousand years old. Egypt's three main pyramid's positions on the ground, along with the southern shaft of the kings chamber in the Great Pyramid, aligns with the Orion constellation dating back to at least 10,400 BC. And this leads one to question; why would the Egyptians spend a massive amount of time and labor to construct three huge monuments of stone just to align them with the Orion constellation almost eight thousand years in their past? Could it be possible that the interpreters are mistaken and those etchings on the wall of the Great Pyramid mark a major event other than the date of its completion?

If the object that was once housed in the stone coffer of the Great Pyramid were to be the same one that was placed in the Ark of the Covenant, then it emitted a powerful source of light because the Bible states that Moses' physical body glowed upon his return form Mount Sinai. Also, the southern shaft of the king's chamber in the Great Pyramid where that stone coffer is located is aimed at the Orion Constellation.

A couple of years ago, I read a news article in which NASA had recalculated the distance from earth to Orion and had discovered that it was not fifteen hundred light-years as previously thought, but instead, it was only *thirteen hundred light-years from earth to the Constellation of Orion.*

So is it possible that the date of 2,600 BC etched on the wall of the Great Pyramid marked the year in which a *light message* was sent to the Orion Constellation, possibly in the form of an SOS? If this were to be correct, then it would've taken that message, traveling at the speed of light, thirteen hundred years to reach Orion. And if whoever received that message were to also be bound by the speed of light then it would've taken another thirteen hundred years for earth to receive a response, either in the form of a message, or by the arrival of someone. And 2,600 BC minus 2,600 years equals the birth of Christ.

But before it can be considered this could've actually happened, there are two major questions that must be answered. First, was the southern shaft of the king's chamber still in alignment with Orion in the year 2,600 BC? And the answer to that is, while it was not in direct alignment, it still pointed to the same immediate vicinity. Therefore, if a message in the form of a powerful beam of light had been sent from the Great Pyramid in 2,600 BC, it certainly would've been visible when it reached Orion thirteen hundred years later. Second, if it was Jesus who responded to that message and came to earth from the Orion Constellation, then why did it take Him another thirteen hundred years to arrive? Since God is the creator of the light, then surely He and Christ are not bound by the law of the speed of light. So, if a Godly entity had responded to that light message once it had reached Orion in 1,300 BC, then there should've been an immediate response, either in the form of a message, or by the arrival of someone.

The Pharaoh Ramses the II ruled Egypt from 1,290 BC till 1,224 BC. It was during this time in which Moses casts ten plagues on Egypt forcing Ramses to set the Israelites free to him. Not only does this Biblically documented event reveal that there was an immediate response to that light message when it reached Orion in 1,300 BC, but that it was answered by none other than the arrival of God Almighty Himself! God worked through Moses to severely punish the Egyptians and force Ramses to set His now chosen people free to him. This also reveals that the light message sent in 2,600 BC was most likely in the form of an SOS.

So maybe that Greek definition of the word pyramid is also wrong; instead of it meaning "visible light measure", maybe it meant *visible light message.*

But Exodus also states that not long after they had been set free and departed Egypt that Ramses suddenly changed his mind and sent sixteen hundred chariots in hot pursuit of the Israelites. This makes one wonder; what could've caused Ramses to do a complete one eighty and chase after them? Is it possible that the God of Moses took something that belonged to Him from that stone coffer of the Great Pyramid at the same time of the Exodus? And is it possible that when Ramses discovered that object was missing, he sent his army after the Israelites, not to return them to Egypt, but instead to retrieve that object?

If there was an object taken from that coffer and placed in the Ark of the Covenant, then according to scripture, it emanated a source of energy so powerful that it was deadly for humans to go near it. And when observing a picture of that empty coffer there is a huge chip on one top corner and the lid to it is missing. And this leads one to conclude that if there was a powerful object kept inside of that coffer, then not only was that object suddenly and hastily removed, but that it also would've required an even more powerful, otherworldly force to be involved in its removal.

When reading the Old Testament, it becomes obvious that this major event also marked the beginning of the final phase of God's plan for the salvation of mankind. The next thirteen hundred years were spent laying the ground work for the arrival of His Son, Jesus.

And not only do these dates, timelines, and events coincide, but one particular number involved with them is also very revealing. First, it took that light message sent from the pyramid *thirteen* hundred years to reach Orion. Second, God responded to that light message in approximately *thirteen* hundred BC. Third, Christ was born *thirteen* hundred years later. And finally, Christ was known as the *thirteenth* apostle.

Chapter 4

The Bible and the Pyramid Connection

It's believed that when pyramid inches are seen as years, the passage of the Great Pyramid becomes a prophetic timeline that coincides with events from the Bible.

The stone coffer in the pyramid has virtually the same cubic capacity of the Ark of the Covenant. Estimating the thickness of the sides of the Ark, it had a total of 71,282 inches while the coffer had a total of 71,250 cubic inches.

The stone coffer and a portion of the floor of the antechamber are made of red granite. Red granite is found on Mount Horeb, which is also believed to be Mount Sinai where Moses received the Ten Commandments.

Revelations 14:3 states "And no man could learn that song but the 144,000 that were redeemed from the earth." The total number of reflective outer casing stones on the Great Pyramid totaled 144,000.

Revelations 4:4 states "And round about the throne were four and twenty elders sitting; clothed in white raiment; and they had on their heads crowns of gold." The main entrance to the Great Pyramid, along with its main passages, are located twenty-four feet east of the center of the pyramid.

Revelations 4:5 states "And out of the throne proceeded lightning and thunder and voices and there were *seven* lamps of fire burning before the throne, which are the *seven* spirits of God." The height of the passageway in the grand galley is *seven* times the average height of the other passages. Its walls consist of *seven* courses of stone. There is a groove on each wall that runs the entire length of the galley that is *seven* inches in height, *one* inch in depth and located *five* inches from the *third* overlapping corbel.

Revelations 13:8 states "Here is wisdom, Let him that hath understanding count the number of the beast; for it is the number of a man; and his number is six hundred threescore and six." If the length of the diagonals in the floor of the antechamber is measured in pyramid inches, they total 666 inches.

John 21:11 states "Simon Peter went up and drew the net to land full of great fishes, *an hundred and fifty-three.*"

The grand galley of the Great Pyramid is one hundred and fifty-three feet long. The total number of steps from the base of the pyramid to its top are one hundred and fifty-three. There are seventeen steps from the pyramids base to its main entrance. One hundred and fifty-three is the seventeenth triangular number, and seventeen is the seventh prime number. One fifty-three is also the sum of the first seventeen natural numbers(i.e. 1+2+3+4 etc.)

Isaiah 19:19 states "In that day there shall be an altar unto the Lord in the midst of the land of Egypt, and a pillar at the border thereof unto the Lord." In 1868, while working on a report for the Suez Canal, Hydrographer "Henry Mitchell" noted that the Nile Delta is pie-shaped and that the Great Pyramid sits in the exact middle bordering upper and lower Egypt.

A Pyramid Based on the Seventeenth Triangular Number

The above triangle is made from 153circles with all three of it's sides consisting of 17 circles for each side.

And it was also learned from my previous writing of the importance of the number thirty-six within the year 2036. There are thirty-six ceiling stones in the grand galley, and it's believed that at one time they were removable which has caused speculation that the Great Pyramid may have been used as an observatory. Also, the entire pyramid was covered with 144,000 casing stones which means there were 36,000 on each of its four sides.

But what makes the pyramid so unique is that its base is a perfect four-sided square and within that square lies the radius of a perfect circle. And that circle is encased by four geometrical triangles perfectly fitted together, and each triangular side of the pyramid is a mirrored reflection of the pyramid itself as a whole.

In Revelation John describes the new Temple as it descends from heaven, stating it will consist of *twelve* foundations, *twelve* gates, *twelve* pearls, and *twelve* angels. It will be *twelve* thousand furlongs square, and its walls will be 144 cubits, which is *twelve* times *twelve*. And on each side of the new Temple will be the names of three of the *twelve* tribes of Israel, which will total 36,000 for each side. And there were 36,000 casing stones on each side of the Great Pyramid. Its apparent twelve will be a vital number concerning the new Temple and new Jerusalem, so is it possible to find this number somewhere within the Great Pyramid?

Since there are four sides to the pyramid, if you do not count its base(floor), and each side is of the same geometrical design, which is that of a triangle that consist of three angles, then maybe they are to be added together. Four sides times three angles equals twelve.

Not only does the number twelve play a vital role in the design of the new Temple and new Jerusalem, but it's also used in other parts of the Bible, such as there being twelve thousand in each of the twelve tribes of Israel. And in the first verse of the twelfth chapter of Revelation, John sees the Virgin Mary wearing a crown of twelve stars. And then there's the fact that there were twelve main apostles.

From previous research, I have learned certain Biblical numbers represent spirits, such as the Seven Spirits of God and the Four Spirits of Christ. Yet, the seven years for the tribulation and the 2012 prophecy contain numbers that are mirrors of one another, such as the numbers twenty-one and twelve, thirty-six and sixty-three, and thirty-seven and seventy-three. From seeing the number twelve's great scriptural importance, I became convinced it held a symbolic Biblical secret. So I spent many hours studying this number in an attempt to unlock the mystery to its great significance. Then one day, just like the Bible states, *"seek and you shall find,"* it was revealed to me. *The number twelve connects the Seven Spirits of God and the Four Spirits of Christ together as one.* But you're not going to have to take my word for it that this is true, for I am going to show it to you in that other language of God, the language of math.

The 7 Spirits of God X 12 = 84 and 8+4 = 12.

The 4 Spirits of Christ X 12 = 48 and 4+8 = 12.

And 1 + 2 = 3 and 1 + 2 = 3 which becomes 33.

Note that the numbers 84 and 48 are mirrors of one another. And when 84 and 48 are added individually, they both add right back to 12.

But that's not all, when the two twelve's are added individually, they each add to 3 which becomes 33. Thirty-three was the age of Christ when He was crucified and resurrected. In the New Testament, Christ stated more than once that He had come from the Father and was of the Father, and therefore, they were One and the Same. And here it is again in God's undeniable language of math. Now it makes perfect sense why there were twelve apostles. There had to be twelve before Christ could connect them to Him and through Him to the Father. And there shouldn't be a need to explain why all those twelve's will be associated with the new Temple and new Jerusalem; that should now be obvious.

I have studied and wondered at length about what will happen to those who know Christ upon the moment He returns. And every time I do, there are two verses that come to mind over and again in which 1 Corinthians 15:51-52 states *"Behold I show you a mystery; We shall not all sleep, but we shall all be changed. In a moment, in the twinkling of an eye, at the last trump:"*

There are three parts that consist in the makeup of a human being, which are the body, the soul, and the spirit. And there are also three known dimensions within the known world. But the number of Spirits of Christ is Four. So when He comes back for those that know Him and they are changed in the twinkling of an eye, will this be the opening of a new dimension; a dimension where life will be perfected and eternal?

Chapter 5

The Number 153

Soon after Christ's resurrection, there is a story in the book of John concerning some of the disciples on a small ship in the sea of Tiberius. The disciples had been fishing, casting out their net all night, but had caught nothing. The next morning they are located two hundred cubits from shore when Jesus appears and calls out to them to cast their net from the right side of their ship; and when they do their net becomes full of fish. At that moment, they recognize that the one on shore is Christ and turn their ship toward Him. Upon their arrival, Jesus instructs them to count the fish they had just caught which came to 153.

This struck me as very odd; this was the last time Jesus was to meet with His disciples before His ascension to Heaven, and they were counting fish? From knowing that certain Biblical numbers have secrets waiting to be revealed, I instantly knew that in much the same way a fisherman would cast out a line hooked with bait, that the last thing Christ had done before He left this world was to toss out the number 153. Therefore, like a fish filled with a hunger from curiosity and a desire to know its hidden mystery, I took that bait and was instantly hooked. For I knew somewhere within that number existed at least a two-thousand-year-old enigma, and just like a treasure hunter who had just discovered a mysterious clue, I knew if I could uncover the secret within it that it would reveal something of a great biblical significance.

Now I was studying the number (153) just as I had previously with the 2012 prophecy, the tribulation, and the number twelve. But this time I had become obsessed. The hidden semblance of what that number meant was all I could think about from that moment forward. But, I was also aware from prior experience that solving and revealing its secret was most likely not going be easy, and that I would once again be burning the midnight oil.

My first approach in an attempt to solve the mystery behind this number was to search the Biblical fish story for other numbers that might reveal an association to 153. The only other number mentioned was the two hundred cubits, so I naturally assumed these two had to be connected; otherwise, what could have been the reason for the story stating how far the ship was from the shore?

But, since it appeared there were no further clues about how these two numbers might be associated to each other, it was now time to search elsewhere. And because of the seemingly mysterious relationship of Biblical numbers, specifically 153 to the Great Pyramid, I knew where I was going to search next. This gave me hope that not only would I be able to solve the mystery behind this number; but also, that it would not take very long, even though that thought seemed a little absurd. I mean, other than the number 153, just what could the Great Pyramid and a net full of fish possibly have in common?

One fifty-three is used many times within the design of the Great Pyramid with one of the main areas being the length of the grand galley that leads to the king's chamber. But perhaps even more important is that there are seventeen steps, which lead up to the Pyramid's main entrance and continuing from that seventeenth step there are a total of 153 steps to its top. Remember, *one hundred and fifty-three is the seventeenth triangular number,* and seventeen is also the seventh prime number. This revealed not only a connection of 153 to seventeen in that together they form a triangle; but that both numbers were also connected to the Great Pyramid because its very design is that of a triangle, which itself is based on those same two numbers.

Christ's mention of one fifty-three is the only time it's spoken of in the Bible, yet this number is found throughout the Great Pyramid, which is also located where the Biblical Exodus took place. Therefore, I was convinced the only option I had left in discovering any clues to this number and its association to Christ would have to lie somewhere within the pyramid.

But after having studied this number and many of the places that it's used throughout the pyramid's design, it finally occurred to me that *153 is the 17th triangular number*, and although 153 is mentioned only once in the Bible, that just maybe a hidden clue to 153 lay within taking a closer look at the number seventeen from a Biblical viewpoint. Seventeen is used thirteen times in scripture, and a few of them are as follows: It's first mentioned in Genesis 7:11 which states that the rains of the great flood began in the second month on the ***seventeenth*** day. The next time is in Genesis 8:4 which states that the Ark landed on Mount Ararat on the ***seventeenth*** day of the ***seventh*** month. And Genesis 37:2 state that Joseph was sold into slavery by his brothers at the age of ***seventeen***. And first Kings 14:21 states that the son of King Solomon ruled over Israel for ***seventeen*** years. And second Kings 13:1 states Jehoahaz also ruled over Israel for ***seventeen*** years.

These verses revealed a possible Biblical semblance in that the number seventeen denoted both the end of an era of time and the beginning of a new age. It was on the seventeenth day of the second month in which the rains began that virtually brought an end to all mankind. Then it was on the seventeenth day of the seventh month that the Ark once again touched ground which marked a new beginning. From now knowing that *one fifty-three is the seventeenth triangular number,* and that both these numbers were used in the design of the Great Pyramid, and that one fifty-three was the last number mentioned by Christ, it was now obvious to me that the Bible, the Great Pyramid, and these numbers were somehow connected. And since the Bible had revealed a pattern of the number seventeen as being a measurement of time, it was beginning to seem as though that *somewhere within the design of the Great Pyramid there existed a hidden calendar.*

And if this happened to be correct, then the unanswered questions were: Where is this calendar located? Would I be able to recognize it and know I had found it? And most importantly, what era of time would it represent? What would be its beginning date and when would it end?

Chapter 6

The Missing Number

The next several days were spent attempting to find a connection to the numbers two hundred, one fifty-three, seventeen, and seven to each another in what surely had to be every conceivable way. Following the same procedure as many scholars, I converted the grand galley from 153 feet to 1,836 inches. I then added, subtracted, divided, and multiplied all the other numbers against 1,836 and each other, but without any success. And even though my conviction that these numbers were somehow connected hadn't wavered any, my confidence that I could solve this puzzle had, because I was beginning to feel overwhelmed and that I was in over my head.

But just when I was about to give up, it occurred to me that one fifty-three is the seventeenth triangular number and that a triangle has three sides, so there had to be a third number. I then simply divided one fifty-three by seventeen and the answer was ***nine.*** I felt the finding of this number was huge, but instead of attempting to solve this triangular riddle by searching the pyramid for a mathematical solution, I decided to do as I had done previously with the number seventeen and search the Bible for a symbolic pattern of the number nine.

And it didn't take long before it was obvious that this number is very prominent when it comes to scripture. It's mentioned many times throughout the Bible. It's used in Genesis in reference to the length of human life in which each of the Bible's earliest patriarchs lived to be approximately *nine hundred* years old. It was in Genesis *9:9* that God established a covenant with Noah following the flood. God established a covenant with Abraham when he was *ninety-nine* years old. In 1 Corinthians, the number of gifts for the first fruits of the spirit is *nine*. Luke 24:44 states that it was in the *ninth* hour that Christ died on the cross. And there is also the fact that the time from the moment of conception until the birth of a human life is normally *nine* months.

From these verses it appeared that the Biblical semblance of the numbers nine and seventeen were similar in that both were often used as forms of measures of time. But, there was a distinct difference in that the number nine was often associated with the creation of a new covenant. So then I became curious to know the total number of covenants there were within the Bible, with the hope that it might reveal another clue.

And as it turned out God's *first covenant* was with Adam and Eve in which they were to be caretakers of the Garden of Eden and not to eat the fruit from the tree of knowledge of good and evil. God's *second covenant* was with Noah immediately following the flood. The *third covenant* was with Abraham; the *fourth covenant* was with Isaac; the *fifth covenant* was with Jacob; the *sixth covenant* was with the Israelites at Mount Sinai; the *seventh covenant* was with David; the *eighth covenant* was Christ's offering of love, forgiveness, and salvation. And the *ninth covenant*, which is yet to happen, was Christ's promise to return with the kingdom yet to come. I was now beginning to sense that I was onto something because not only was the number nine following a pattern as a Biblical measurement of time, but there also existed a total of nine covenants in which all had been fulfilled except for the last one.

Therefore, I couldn't help but recall from my previous writing in which it was revealed the great significance of the number nine and its prominence within both the seven years of the tribulation and the 2012 prophecy. In that writing, it was learned that the Antichrist will enter Jerusalem in the year 2033, which will be the dawning of the third day in the realm of God. Revelation then states three and one half years later he will enter the new temple which will be in the year 2036. And when these numbers are seen as spirits and added together(which is simply $3+6 = 9$), they revealed that the moment the Antichrist takes possession of that holy ground he will attempt to become 9 evil spirits.

Revelation 16:13 states "And I saw three evil spirits that looked like frogs; they came out of the mouth of the dragon, out of the mouth of the beast, and out of the mouth of the false prophet," and this totals to 9 evil spirits. Revelation then states that these spirits go about performing great miracles in their attempts to gather support for their impending battle with Christ. Therefore, because many nations will be deceived by these miracles, those nations will believe they are aiding Christ in defeating Satan but, in reality, they unknowingly will be helping Satan in his attempt to defeat Christ.

But that's not all; when the numbers that are mirrors of one another within the date of the 2012 prophecy are added together and then their totals are seen as spirits, they also add up to nine.

First, the numbers that mirror one another within the *date* of *12-21*-20*12*.

$1+2 = (3)$ $2+1 = (3)$ $1+2 = (3)$ and $3+3+3 = $ **9**.

And then the three twelves within the number of *12*-21-*2012* were added together.

$12+12+12 = (36)$ and $3+6 = $ **9**.

Next; the mirrors of the three twelve's, the three twenty-ones were added together.

$21+21+21 = (63)$ and $6+3 = $ **9**.

Also note that the three twelve's total to (36), and that the three twenty-ones equal to (63), and that these numbers are also mirrors of one another.

In the beginning of the Bible, each patriarch died after having lived approximately (*nine*) hundred years, which marked the end of an era that was followed by a new beginning. It was right after the flood in Genesis chapter *nine* verse *nine* in which a covenant marked the end of an era and the start of a new beginning. Abraham, at the age of *ninety-nine,* entered into a covenant that was the start of God's plan of salvation, which marked the end of an era followed by a new beginning. Christ died on the cross in the *ninth* hour; therefore, it also marked the end of an era and the beginning of a new age.

In seeing the semblance of the number nine's association to the covenants throughout the history of the Biblical past, one can also see its semblance will be the same for the Biblical future. The *nines* in the 2012 prophecy, along with the *nine* evil spirits in Revelation, and the *nine* in the year 2036 reveal that the *ninth* covenant will soon be fulfilled by the ending of this current era and the beginning of a new age; *an age that will be marked by the return of Christ.*

But even as astounding as this is, the most important revelation for the moment may be that the number nine is also the Bible's marker for time itself. What is meant by this is even though the Bible marked time by counting generations, the precise number of years that consist of a single Biblical generation has never been established. And although those earliest patriarchs lived to be nearly nine hundred years old, it's most likely they lived for many generations; and therefore, their life span did not constitute how many years there are in a single generation. What has been the accepted belief among some Biblical scholars is that a generation consists of forty years, which is attributed to the length of time an evil generation of Israelites were led around in the desert. But what the Bible is really stating is how long that generation was led around in the desert and not how many years there are in a generation.

So the unanswered question has always been; what is the precise number of years that would constitute a single Biblical generation by God's measure? In seeing how the number nine marks the end of Biblical eras of time then it's possible that it also marks the number of years for a single Biblical generation. And if this were to be correct, then nine is merely a base number whose multiplier would need to also have the number nine within its total. Therefore a Biblical generation would have to consist of either 90, 99, 900, or 999 years.

But just as important is, that since nine and seventeen are Biblical measures of time and these numbers are found within the design of the *Great Pyramid,* then one fifty-three must also be a Biblical measure of time. Therefore I felt that either one or both seventeen and one fifty-three held the secret to finding the correct multiplier of nine, which would in turn reveal the correct number of years for a single Biblical generation.

Now I had before me a puzzle that consisted of the numbers one fifty-three, seventeen, and nine with the only clue being that they might possibly somehow form a triangular-shaped calendar.

But I also knew that if this puzzle was going to be solved that I would need to find that multiplier of nine, which would reveal the correct number of years for a single generation.

Therefore many hours were spent searching these numbers, the Bible, and the pyramid for a connection of them to the number nine, which would reveal the multiplier for a single generation, but without any success.

Then it finally occurred to me that the answer that I sought may lie within what was revealed from my previous book in knowing that Christ will return in the year 2040 and that it will be the final year of the last generation. I was now convinced that upon subtracting units of nine from the year 2040 that one of them was going to reveal a dated biblical event which would connect that unit of nine to either the number one fifty-three or seventeen as to being the correct number of years for a single biblical generation.

And when ninety years was subtracted from the year 2040, the answer was the year 1950. From knowing that one fifty-three is the last number mentioned by Christ; and, that it's the seventeenth triangular number; and, that both are found within the design of the Great Pyramid, a dated biblical event was needed to connect ninety years to either one or both the numbers one fifty-three, and or seventeen.

And when *seventeen* years was added to 1950, the answer was the year *1967.* This is the year in which the Israelites won their Six-Day War against Egypt, Syria, Jordan, and Iraq. But even more important is that for the first time in almost 1,900 years they also reclaimed their ancient city of Jerusalem. And this event is both Biblical and historical.

This revealed several things at once. First, it revealed that not only the numbers 153, 17, and 9 are connected in a Biblical sense, but that they also show a related pattern within the very design of the Great Pyramid; therefore, the connection of these numbers to the Bible and the pyramid cannot be considered a mere coincidence. Second, it's now known for the first time in history that a Biblical generation consists of ninety years. Third, those born in the year 1950 and later are of the final generation. Fourth, it further substantiated the revelation from my previous book that Christ will return in the year 2040.

But the most important revelation for the moment was knowing that a single Biblical generation consisted of ninety years. And, since this number is related to one fifty-three and seventeen and all three numbers are found within the design of the Great Pyramid; not only was I now convinced that a calendar existed somewhere within the pyramid, but also, that it was *a **Biblical calendar.***

And in knowing this, I couldn't help but recall that biblical verse from an earlier chapter in which comparisons were made between scripture and the Great Pyramid. Again, Isaiah chapter *nine*-teen, verse *nine*-teen states, "In that day there shall be an altar to the Lord in the midst of the land of Egypt."

Chapter 7

Assembling the Calendar

From knowing that ninety years was the length for a Biblical generation and from seeing its close relation to the number seventeen in both the Bible and within the design of Great Pyramid, I was now convinced ninety years had to be a Biblical measurement of time within the pyramid's calendar. So, the next question became; just what was the number seventeen's relation to the number nine in the counting of these generations? In seeing the Biblical semblance of these two numbers it was apparent they both were measures of time. And with this in mind, I then multiplied ninety years times seventeen and received the answer of 1,530 years.

This led me to believe that seventeen generations at ninety years for each generation marked the end of an era and the beginning of a new age. And if this were to be correct, then it was also possible that every seventeenth generation or every 1,530 years would complete one level of the pyramid calendar. In going forward with this presumption the next questions became how many levels would there be to this calendar, and what era of time would it measure? Or as stated earlier, when did it start, and when will it end?

The final clue left to be answered in an attempt to solve this puzzle was the same number that was responsible for the start of this search. I now felt for sure that ninety years equaled one generation and that seventeen generations completed one level of the pyramid calendar; therefore, one fifty-three had to hold the secret to both the total number of levels and the total number of years for the whole calendar.

Therefore, one fifty-three had to be merely a base number that would need a multiplier totaling more than 1,530. But, I was also convinced that the resulting total from that multiplier would have to include the number 153 within it.

Immediately I thought of the Biblical fish story and was sure the two hundred cubits had to be the correct multiplier of one fifty-three, but 153 times 200 comes to 30,600 years, and I felt this was the wrong multiplier for two reasons. First, it did not contain the number 153 within its total, and second, most Biblical scholars believe creation began around 4,000 BC, which puts the current age of the Biblical world at approximately 6,000 years old.

Since the two hundred cubits wasn't the multiplier, and there were no other numbers mentioned in the fish story, it was now time to search for that multiplier in the only other place it could be, within the Great Pyramid. The length of the grand galley is one hundred and fifty-three feet, and to make a long search short, located at its top is the so-called king's chamber in which the total number of stones that make up its four wall consist of precisely one hundred blocks.

And one fifty-three multiplied by one hundred comes to 15,300 years. I felt this to be the correct multiplier because not only did this number have one fifty-three in its total, but it was also a more workable number in estimating what's perceived to be the true age of the biblical world. Now, not only did I feel that this was the correct number of years for the length of the calendar, but I was also beginning to conceive of the notion that regardless of its beginning date, its ending date was going to reveal the end of time.

And as a result from feeling that I was on the right path, I was now ready to attempt to add up all the years from the beginning of the Biblical creation till the year 2011 with the hope that it would give a ball park estimate of how much time, if any, would be left on the calendar.

Most scholars believe the Biblical world to be approximately six thousand years old. But, I personally take issue with this figure because this estimate is based on the book of Genesis stating that God created the world in six days, and these scholars believe Genesis is referring to six earth days.

But 2 Peter 3:8 states *"But beloved, be not ignorant of this one thing, that one day is with the Lord as a thousand years, and a thousand years as one day."*

So depending on how one interprets Genesis, it could've just as easily taken God six thousand years to create this world. And besides, a true artist is never in a hurry, but takes his time, taking great pleasure in what he creates; and also, God is not bound by time; therefore, He has forever to perfect His creation of this world. And still yet, there also remains that question about the true age of the pyramids. Again, why would the ancient Egyptians align them with the Orion Constellation to at least 8,000 years in their past?

Since Genesis states that Adam was created on the sixth day or (in the six thousandth year), then the next step in acquiring an estimate of the current age of the Biblical world lay within the number of years between the creation of Adam until the birth of Christ. One might assume all the generations spoken of in the Old Testament times ninety would reveal a fair assessment as to the number of years from the creation of Adam until the arrival of Christ. But, as previously mentioned, the Bible only counted years when it came to the life span of its patriarchs; and, those earliest patriarchs lived for many generations. Furthermore, when it comes to the Old Testament, it's believed some generations were overlooked altogether.

But in the New Testament, the book of Luke lists the names of the sons from Adam till the birth of Christ which totals to seventy-six. And even though there isn't any way of knowing just how long each son lived or taking into account the length of life of those earlier patriarchs, this still made for a fair gauge in estimating the number of years between the creation of Adam until the birth of Christ simply by multiplying ninety years times seventy-six which came to 6,840 years.

Now it was time to add all these years together and get a total. Six thousand years for creation, plus six thousand eight hundred and forty years from Adam until the birth of Christ added up to 12,840 years, plus the age of Christ at the time of His ascension of thirty-three came to 12,873 years, plus 2,011 years gave a final total of 14,884 years. And although this is just an estimate, if 15,300 were to be the correct number of years for the length of the calendar then it would be safe to say that it's not far from its expiration date.

Having determined that one generation consist of ninety years, and that seventeen generations, or every 1,530 years completed one level of the pyramid calendar, and that 15,300 years was the length of time for the entire calendar, now made it possible to put these numbers in their proper numerical positions within the pyramid and for the first time to actually see the calendar.

The 15, 300 Year Pyramid Calendar

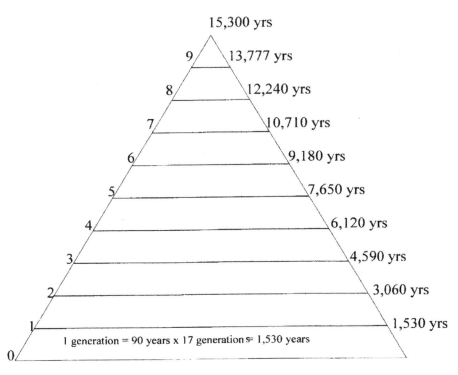

Because it's presumed this is a Biblical calendar which measures time from the moment of creation then it must begin at zero. Seventeen generations at ninety years per generation equals 1,530 years for each level of the pyramid calendar. And if the previous estimate of 14,884 is anywhere close to being a fair assessment of how many years have already passed, then one can easily see that this calendar is very near its end.

But, a Biblically associated event and number is still needed to mark this calendar with a specific amount of years in order to determine its beginning and ending dates. Achieving that would not only confirm it as a Biblical calendar that is measuring the length of time from the beginning of the Biblical creation until the end of time, but it would also give a more precise measurement of how many years are left until its conclusion.

It was obvious that a biblical event and number were not going to be easy to find, but I knew where I was going to search first. I was still convinced those two hundred cubits in the fish story held a secret to this calendar. But at the same time, I also knew I didn't have the first clue about how or where to apply that number to the calendar. Therefore it appeared it was time for me to go out and buy more oil for that midnight lamp.

Chapter 8

A Very Perplexing Clue

The same night I finished the previous chapter, I settled down to relax in front of the TV with my favorite snack consisting of a peanut butter sandwich and a diet coke. After random channel surfing, I decided on an episode of "Legend Quest" in which they were searching for, of all things, Kings Solomon's ring. No one can say that the ring ever really existed; it's considered to be a legend in which the ring was a gift from God that gave Solomon magical powers over demons. And while I was interested in the search for the ring, I was tired from working on the book and was finding it hard to stay awake and pay attention. However, as the show came to its conclusion, there was a video of the Pope wearing a gold ring on his finger. And as the host was leaving the viewers with the unanswered question as to whether or not this could possibly be the legendary ring of Solomon, the camera began slowly zooming in on the ring.

And as it came closer into view, I suddenly saw on its flat surface an engraved image, an image that made me no longer care whether or not the ring was real. An image that jolted me so wide awake that I couldn't have become anymore alert than if someone had just slapped my face to wake me up.

There upon the surface of the ring was an image of two pyramids intersecting each other with their tips pointing in opposite directions.

I immediately and instinctively felt this had to be one of those subtle clues from God and I had almost missed it. But moreover, that emblem on the Pope's ring is not uniquely rare. In fact it's known in geometry as a hexagram and widely recognized the world over as the "Star of David" and is even the official symbol for the nation of Israel. Therefore I couldn't help but berate myself for not having recalled or taken prior notice of that emblem, much less that it was painfully apparent that God had to virtually stick the Pope's finger through the TV and into my face to make me aware of it.

And as exciting as it was to have this new clue, even though it had almost poked me in the eye, it only raised many questions while answering nothing. Did this mean there was a second individual calendar; or were there two connected calendars, such as a calendar within a calendar; or were they just two connected pyramids that had nothing to do with a calendar? In order to find possible answers to these questions, I began searching the history of the emblem.

According to legend, it was not the ring that held the power to control demons, but rather the emblem itself, which was referred to as the *seal* of Solomon. But once Solomon died, the ring and its emblem seemed to have just disappeared, only for the emblem to suddenly resurface in Rabbinic literature during the Middle Ages. But now the emblem is no longer attributed to Solomon, and instead, is now referred to as the "Star of David." And it seems this came about from a Jewish midrash (legend) in which David, while in a duel with King Nimrod, used a round shield that was reinforced from behind with two intersecting triangles. The legend states that at one point the duel between David and Nimrod became so intense that the two triangles became fused together, strengthening David's shield protecting and aiding him in his victory. As a result, the two triangles became known as the *"Shield of David."* Jewish Kabbalists (mystics) began associating the symbol with a deeper spiritual meaning and therefore it became a trademark among the Jewish people with the emblem appearing on many Jewish buildings. And, it was because of the Jews' association with this symbol that during WWII Hitler made them wear it as a badge of shame. Then once the war was over and the Jews had migrated back to their homeland of Israel, they adopted the emblem as their national symbol.

Over time other theories also evolved about the semblance of the emblem, such as its six points referring to God watching over the six positions of the earth (east, west, north, south, upper, and lower), or its twelve sides representing the original twelve tribes of Israel.

And while all this made for very interesting reading, these stories only amounted to legends, filled with speculative theories, and none of them held a single clue about why the emblem consisted of two intersecting pyramids, which left the hunt for the true origin of the emblem and its meaning at a virtual dead end.

This left me disappointed and confused; I was positive the emblem was a clue. I even thought it possibly held the key to a Biblical event and year that would mark the precise length of time of the pyramid calendar. But how was I to find the meaning of the emblem, much less attach a date to it, if it only existed in what appeared to be mythical legends? And even those stories provided no insight to the true meaning of the emblem. And moreover, why would God put a clue right under my nose just for it to lead to a dead end; Or, maybe I was mistaken, and this was not even a clue, but instead was just a mere coincidence?

After having taking all this into consideration, it seemed the only option I had left, at least for the moment, was to return to searching for a biblical event with a date or number that would connect it to the calendar, while trusting in that old cliché that God works in mysterious ways, and if this were to be a clue, then when the time was right, it would be revealed to me.

The next several days were filled with long hours of attempting to find the elusive Biblical event that would reveal a number which would date the calendar. In fact, the search was expanded to include anything mentioned within scripture associated with a number; such as, the ages of the lives of patriarchs, or the number of a verse that spoke of a major event, or any numbers associated with an event, and even the number of a verse that mentioned any numbers within that particular verse. And as this search wore on, I began to feel as though I was either searching for the proverbial needle in a haystack or for something that simply just did not exist.

Suffering from mental exhaustion and frustration, I decided it was time to take a break and get away from all these verses, dates, events, and numbers. The following week was spent catching up on yard work, housework, washing clothes, paying bills, washing the car, getting a haircut, etc. But even while pretending to be preoccupied with those distractions, I constantly thought about that elusive event and number that would date the calendar. Where could it be? Had I overlooked it? Did it even exist? Once again I was beginning to feel overwhelmed, and therefore convinced that if it did exist I was going to need help finding it from an other worldly source.

Chapter 9

The Dream

The clock on the night stand to the right of my bed had been silenced from its angry demands that I arise to go to work since my retirement in 2008. Therefore, my eyes opened to the sound of silence, and needless to say, it's a wonderful way to awake from a night's sleep. Upon awakening, I became aware I was lying on my left side and turning to my right from curiosity to know the current time, I saw the clock's huge green luminescent digits displaying 6:23 a.m. If not for the fact that I was now retired, I would've already been over a half hour late for work. But since there was nowhere I had to be, 6:23 a.m. was just too early to rise, so I attempted to will myself back to sleep, but to no avail. Giving up and once again opening my eyes, I found myself face-to-face with the clock, which now read 6:33 a.m.

Turning over onto my back, I began debating on whether or not to get up and start my day while staring up at the ceiling fan and observing the continuous spin of its blades as they traveled around in a blurry circle above me. And then I began playing one of those little mind games that I do from time to time as I wondered, was it possible to focus on a single blade of that fan and not lose sight of it within the blurred motion of the others? I locked my eyes on to one as it made its way around the ceiling and watched it for several revolutions while never allowing it to skewer from my view. It wasn't long before I had decided this little eye test was just too easy; but for whatever reason, I just kept lying there staring up at the continuous blur of those swirling blades, and my mind wandered to that elusive number I needed to date the calendar. My brain became filled with dates, numbers, verses, and events as I began recalling them into my memory to reinsure myself I hadn't overlooked anything.

But, in much the same way someone would erase dates, numbers, and events from a chalkboard, all my thoughts began to melt away into nothing, leaving my mind blank. And even though I was vaguely aware that I was still physically lying in my bed, I was also, at that same moment, acutely aware that I was somewhere I had never been before.

At first I felt as though my mind, or leastwise my imagination, had to be playing a trick on me because I was now standing on what appeared to be a seashore. To my right was a large body of water, which I naturally assumed to be an ocean. Directly out in front of me, I could see tiny ripples of waves racing one behind the other up onto the sands of the beach, and the shoreline continued on for as far as I could see.

At the same point on the horizon where the sky met the shore, I began a slow visual panning to my left. And as I did this, my view became obscured by a forest of tall trees thickly layered with leaves and foliage which began about forty yards inward from the shore and about one hundred yards away from me. And, as I continued to look around to my left the wall of trees fanned out into what was similar to that of a half circle obscuring my ability to see beyond; and, by the time I had turned my head to the point of looking directly off my left shoulder, they were a good seventy to eighty yards away and the sun was rising above them.

It was my intention to keep turning to my left until I had turned a full 360 degrees, but at that precise moment a soft gentle breeze began to blow from behind me continuing straight down the shoreline, and in that same instant (and I can't explain this) from somewhere deep inside of me I somehow knew that looking behind me was strictly forbidden.

Knowing that turning around was out of the question, I began searching for a break in the trees that would allow me to see what they were obviously hiding from my sight, but without any success. So, I then considered walking the seventy or so yards over to them in an attempt to see through; but just like before, somehow I instinctively knew it was forbidden; and in that instant, I also sensed that the purpose for my being there was to stand still and observe.

Thus, I began slowly panning my way back around to my right toward the direction of the ocean all the while searching for a break within trees with the hope that at some point I might be able to see beyond. But at about the half way point in which the trees were the furthest from me, I saw the image of a man appear from out of the midst of the foliage and, it seemed as though he were walking toward me, therefore I was certain he was there to explain to me why I was there.

As he came closer, I could see that he was dressed in a long pristine white robe and had light brown shoulder length hair, a matching beard, carrying a fishing line in his left hand; and, attached to the end of it were several fish. He was about fifty yards away from me when he suddenly stopped, turned, and faced the ocean. I then heard him call out, "Children, have you any meat?" And when I turned and looked there on the water about three hundred feet from shore was a tiny ship not much larger than a boat. And on its deck, I saw the silhouettes of four or five men with their hands cupped just above their eyes, blocking the glare of the morning sun in an attempt to see who had called out to them. One of the men yelled, "no," to which the one on shore replied; "Cast your net from the right side of the ship and ye shall find."

And in that moment I knew that the Biblical story of the one hundred and fifty-three fish was taking place right in front of me, and in that same instant, I heard a voice, (but not via a sound in my ear but in my mind, literally, telepathically,) which asked, *"When He first met them He instructed them in this same manner, so what is the difference in that moment and in this moment?"*

I continued watching the men on the deck of the ship as they gathered and readied their net to cast into the water, and I thought back to that story of their first meeting, recalling that the net had broken and that the difference was this time it hadn't. Instantly, the voice asked another question, *"Why is it that in both stories, the fish are found on the right side of the ship?"*

As this question was being asked, I observed the men as they cast out their net from the ship, watching it as it splashed onto the surface of the water, then quickly sinking beneath. I'm embarrassed to admit it now, but my first natural thought was, *"because that was the side the fish were on."* And that thought was met with silence; no response was sent back to me and I was left with nothing but a quiet empty mind.

After several moments of thoughtful reflection about why the fish were always on the right side of the ship, it suddenly occurred to me. Although the two stories were similar, they also contained subtle differences; and within those differences there existed yet a third symbolic story with a deeper meaning. Now I knew not to perceive them as separate stories but to search for the subtle differences and symbolisms within the two.

With this revelation, the answer to the previous question came quickly to me and I answered, *"those who have received salvation through Christ will be on the right come judgment day."* Instantly the voice asked the next question, ***"When He first met them, what did He tell them He would make of them?"***

Suddenly the small ship was literally yanked and made to lean heavily toward its right side and I knew they had just filled their net with one hundred and fifty-three fish. *"He told them He would make them fishers of men,"* was my response. Which was followed by, ***"Why did the first net break?"*** To which I replied, *"because Jesus had not yet completed the plan of salvation, and they were not yet disciples."* Then came the next question, ***"Yet the second time the net held, so what is the semblance of the net and the fish?"***

"The net represents salvation cast into the sea of humanity, and the fish represents the souls of those that receive Christ and therefore are gathered into the net." Immediately came the next question, ***"How long will the net be cast before the ship turns toward the shore, and how long before the ship reaches the shore?"***

The tiny ship was now anchored a few yards from the beach and I could see the men dragging their full net from the shallow water up onto the sand while the one who had called out to them was busy cooking the fish He'd brought with Him over hot coals. *This time I was mentally stumped;* I thought for several moments while watching the men as they spread their net out on the beach and began counting and placing the fish they had just caught into straw baskets which had been retrieved from the ship. I finally had to mentally admit to myself that I did not know how long the net would be cast, or how long it would be until the ship would reach the shore, and in that instant, I heard the next question;

"Upon His resurrection and even now when they first see Him, they do not recognize Him, and when He called out to them from the shore He referred to them as children, why?"

Now all the men from the boat were seated in a circle around the hot coals, eating fish, and listening to the one in white as He spoke to them.

"The disciples failed to understand that once Christ had fulfilled God's plan of salvation, it was now possible for the Father to join

the Son and become as one with Him in the flesh. Therefore when the disciples looked into those now seemingly deep and mysterious eyes of Christ, they did not comprehend that they were also gazing straight into the very eyes of God."

"Why did He ask Peter three times if he loved Him?" *"Each time that Peter spoke from his heart saying yes, it was his unknowing atonement for denying Him three times."*

"And each time Peter replied yes, why did He tell Peter to feed His lambs and His sheep?" *"He was telling Peter that he was no longer a fisherman of the sea, but a fisher of men, and that he was to go forth spreading His gospel to the people thereby insuring that it would also be spread to future generations."*

The men arose from their meal and began picking up the straw baskets filled with fish and I knew they were leaving, but moreover, I instinctively knew it also meant this dream was about to end. My mind raced back to that one question that I could not answer, and I thought to myself, *"how long would the net be cast?"* And immediately I heard the voice again, which asked, **"What is the number of the one in white?"**

Acutely aware my question had been answered with a question and relying on what I learned from the writing of my previous book, I quickly responded, *"four"* to which I instantly heard, **"And in the Old Testament?"** Again, I quickly replied "forty" which was followed with, **"In this manner, perceive the two hundred cubits."**

I then waited for the next question but nothing came to me. I could see the one in white disappearing back into the foliage from whence He came and the others had picked up the baskets of fish and were following single file behind Him. I began to feel a state of panic wash over me. Somehow I instinctively knew when that last disciple disappeared within the trees I was going to wake up, yet there was something missing, questions I hadn't thought of but needed to ask. I watched as the next to the last disciple vanished from my view, only one left before I would wake up; my mind was spinning wildly as I desperately struggled to focus on those questions before it would be too late. *What was I meant to ask!*

In the same moment as that last disciple was fading from my sight within the foliage, it suddenly hit me and in my mind, I hurriedly screamed out the questions; *the calendar? an event? a date? a number? . . .* I waited, hoped, and strained to hear a response, but all I heard was silence.

Once again I was alone on the shore, and the gentle breeze that had been coming from behind me changed direction and began blowing from left to right increasingly harsher, which caused the once perfect scene in front of me to begin to lose its focus as it became more and more distorted. And as the wind increased in its velocity, the ocean, the beach, and the trees were reduced to shapeless colors of swirling shades of blue, green, and beige, which created a whirlwind that continued to grow until it had completely surrounded and engulfed me. At that moment I was convinced my questions had came too late, *but then once again I heard the voice, which faintly said,* **"That which is sought lies within the one who first appeared on the shore."**

And with that the only color left still swirling wildly around me was that blurry shade of beige that had once been the beach, and not wanting to let go of the dream I desperately focused in on it, trying with all my might to mentally will it back into its former shape. But then I slowly began to realize this color was no longer out in front of me but instead, was over me, and that I was awake and staring at nothing more than the beige blades from the ceiling fan as they swirled around in a blurry circle above me.

It could be said it was because of my thirty years of waking up to it's alarm that I instinctively looked to my right to check the current time, and it can even be said that what I saw was a mere coincidence. But I believe it came from a higher designed purpose that I should at that very moment turn and see that clock, for its huge green luminescent digits read **7:17** a.m. Upon seeing those numbers, I immediately recalled that the number of the Spirits of God are **7**, and that **153** is the **17th** triangular number, and that **17** is also the **7th** prime number. And while it may never be known who actually built the Great Pyramid, I was now convinced its design came from the very same entity that's referred to in the Holy Bible as God.

With renewed energy brought on by excitement from the clues revealed in the dream it was time to shower, shave, grab a cup of coffee, a calculator, and get back to solving this puzzle.

Chapter 10

"Seek and Ye Shall Find"

From the very start of this search, the two hundred cubits had frustrated me in much the same way as one who has repeatedly picked up the same piece to a puzzle believing it fit in a certain spot only to realize for the twentieth time that it didn't; But, the dream had revealed a major clue, which was to perceive the two hundred cubits as I would Christ's number of *forty* and *four* in the Old and New Testaments.

I had learned from my previous writing that God's and Christ's numbers change by a multiplier of ten between the Testaments. Twice in the Old Testament God used the number seventy when He was about to move upon the nation of Israel, yet Revelation states His number of Spirits are seven. The other number used twice in the Old Testament was the number forty, and both times it represented a cleansing of evil. And according to Revelation, it will be Christ who will rapture the righteous from an evil world only to bring them back later to a cleansed planet. And forty is closely related to Christ in the New Testament. The first time was that upon being baptized, He spent forty days in the desert, fasting and being tempted by Satan. The second time being that it was forty days between His resurrection and ascension. And still yet, there is also a verse in Revelation which states the number of spirits of Christ are Four. Revelation 5:6 "And I beheld in the midst of the throne and of the *four beasts*; and in the midst of the elders stood a lamb as it had been slain."

And as the voice in my dream had stated, it was now time to mathematically perceive the two hundred cubits in the same manner, which was to simply multiply it by ten.

The first part of the question had been; "how long would the net be cast before the ship would turn toward the shore." Ten times two hundred equals two thousand, and since this number is a reference to how long the net of salvation would be cast into the sea of humanity, then two thousand had to be the number of years. Now I knew that God's plan of salvation would be offered for two thousand years and then things would begin to wrap up very quickly for the return of Christ.

The second part of the question had been; "once the ship turned toward the shore, how long would it be until it arrived?" Since the ship is now headed in the direction of where Christ is located in the story, then it's His number times ten that will reveal how long it will take for the ship to come ashore. And four times ten equals forty, and two thousand years plus forty years equals the year *2040.*

I was dumbstruck as I pushed my chair back away from my desk in amazement. I couldn't get over how frustrated I had become in my attempts to decipher the secret to the two hundred cubits, but now that it had been solved, it seemed almost too simplistic in the beauty of its own truth. But what astounded me most was that in my previous book, it was at Mount Sinai in which I had gone forward in time searching for His lost Ark and had it revealed to me that Christ would return in the year 2040. And in this book, I had come back to Mount Sinai and had traveled backward in time and it hadn't mattered; either way, His truth was the same.

Recalling the sudden increase of natural disasters and violence that has taken place around the world since the year two thousand, I began to see how it made perfect sense in that being the year in which the ship had turned toward the shore.

But, there was still one last huge piece of this puzzle to solve, which was to find a Biblically associated event and number that would precisely mark the length of time for the pyramid calendar. The last statement from the dream had said, "That which is sought lies within the one who first appeared on the shore." Therefore, it seemed in much the same way as the numbers four and forty were the keys to solving the mystery of the two hundred cubits; they were once again going to be the key in finding the number which would mark the calendar. And, for some odd reason, I couldn't help but recall that during His teachings, Jesus had stated more than once that He was the answer; and, how ironic it was that even now in solving this puzzle, He was once again going to be the answer.

But, what I had thought would take only a few minutes to a few hours to solve was far from the truth. I spent the next two days from 9:00 a.m. until 9:00 p.m. trying in every conceivable way to connect forty and four to the calendar. But, I found no date or number that even came close to convincing me it was the correct one. I even tossed the two hundred cubits into the mix hoping that it also played a part in solving this final puzzle, but without any success.

At approximately 1:30 p.m. on the afternoon of the third day, I pushed my swivel chair back away from my desk. Feeling completely frustrated and filled with despair, I swirled around and literally leapt out of my seat and proceeded to stomp down the stairs. Continuing through the living room into the kitchen, I got a diet coke, slammed the refrigerator door, and headed for the back porch. Grabbing a patio chair, I plopped down while twisting off the cap to the soda, and upon taking a quick swig, I frustratingly snapped the bottle away from my lips too soon splashing soda up my nose and onto my face. This left me wondering why I hadn't thought my feelings of frustration and exasperation weren't already enough, why did I have to add self-inflicted idiocy to the mixture?

Weather-wise, it was a glorious day with the sun peaking at me from the top left corner of the house and partially hidden behind a huge white puffy cloud as it lazily wafted by. Attempting to mentally distract myself, I observed a squirrel as it scampered about, digging in the yard, and I wondered, was he hiding food for the upcoming winter, or was he just merely scrounging up something for that evening's supper.

But this feeble attempt fell way short of those overwhelming feelings of exasperation which were now starting to turn to hopelessness. I felt like maybe it was time to give up, because not only could I not find that number for the calendar; but, I also couldn't distinguish whether the hexagram had been a clue or a coincidence. Looking once again in the direction of the sun, which was now completely hidden by the cloud, I did the only thing I felt was left for me to do; I prayed, and it went something like this.

Lord I'm truly thankful for all the great things You have revealed in calling me back to Exodus and the Great Pyramid. But, Lord I am also at a crossroads and ready to accept that what I'm searching for now either does not exist, or it's not meant for me to know. I truly felt You had given me a clue in the dream which I was to search for Your truth and solve this puzzle. But I have tried the numbers four and forty everyway I know possible, and since those numbers are the only two that concern Your Son, . . . or, . . . are they?

In that instant it dawned on me that not once had I considered the notion that four and forty were not the correct numbers to date the calendar, or that there possibly existed another number which might be the correct one. I frantically began searching my memory for other numbers associated with Christ. And then in much the same way a slot machine would stop on its first number, then its second, and finally the third, so did the numbers in my mind. I knew I had found what I had been searching for, . . . *I had my answer!*

Chapter 11

The Number and the Calendar Revealed

I quickly made my way back up the stairs and to the large calculator lying on my desk. Picking it up, I hastily began pushing its huge numerical buttons in an attempt to subtract my newly found number from 15,300. But my hands were shaking from nervous excitement and all I had for fingers were thumbs; therefore, I frustratingly had to clear the numbers out and start over. Making myself go slower, I gradually and deliberately entered the digits and was finally able to force 15,300 onto the calculator's screen and then pushed the minus button. Now it was time to subtract that all elusive number from 15,300, which should reveal a number associated with a Biblical event that would mark the calendar's beginning and ending dates.

I punched in the first number which was 13—(*Christ was the thirteenth apostle*); followed by the second which was 33—(*His age of crucifixion, resurrection, and ascension*); and finally, the number 3—(*He arose on the third day*); or 13,333 and then slowly pushed the equal button.

Inhaling a long deep breath, I stared in complete and total awe at the numbers that appeared before me. It's a good thing that breathing is a natural bodily function, because my brain ceased all activity; and, I held that breath for so long I became dizzy. If my body hadn't taken over forcing me to exhale, I may have, in that moment, suffocated myself.

There on the calculator's screen before me were the numbers *1967: The year the Israelites reclaimed their ancient and holy city of Jerusalem.*

I knew all the many things that had been revealed to me up to this point were nothing short of astounding; but, I also knew that what I had just found was nothing less than what a treasure seeker would refer to as the mother lode! For, I had just unraveled a 2000-year-old hidden secret that mathematically connected Christ and the Bible to the Great Pyramid. Feeling totally overwhelmed and with tears in my eyes all I could do was say to myself over and again, "this was it, this was the main thing that He had wanted me to find.

But upon finally getting control of my faculties once more, immediately a huge question arose; this calendar had already expired because it was now the year 2011. So the question became, just what had this calendar marked? And the answer lay within its expiration date of 1967.

Twice in the Old Testament, God used seventy years when He dealt with the Israelites. And the second time was when *they were given seventy years to recognize Christ as their Messiah after His ascension to Heaven.* And when they failed to do so, *God had their second Temple destroyed.*

My previous writing revealed the year 2033 to be the start of the tribulation in which the Antichrist will enter and occupy Jerusalem. And according to Revelation, he will wait three and one half years while a temple is built for him on the very same spot where that previous temple was destroyed seventy years after Christ's ascension back to Heaven. Therefore, when the Antichrist enters that temple in 2036, it will mark the beginning of the wrath of God by the destruction of that temple in 2037.

So when Christ's number of 13,333 was subtracted from the 15,300 year calendar, it marked two future events. First, it marked the very year the Israelites would reclaim their holy city of Jerusalem in 1967. Second, it marked in years the precise length of time between the destruction of the previous Temple that existed during the time of Christ until the destruction of the next Temple. And, that previous Temple was destroyed *seventy years* after Christ's ascension to Heaven, *and 1967 years plus seventy years equals the year 2037.*

Just as it has been done in their past, the moment Israel was allowed to enter that sacred city of Jerusalem in 1967, they were given seventy years to come back to God and accept Christ as their Messiah. But this time it's a little different, because this seventy years is a final countdown. Not just for Israel, but for the whole world to come back to God or face His wrath in 2037. After all, Revelation also states that the earth must be cleansed of all evil before Christ can return with the righteous in Him in the year 2040.

I had no idea when I began this book that it was going to take me to the very same year as my last book, which was 2037. Now as I ask myself, I will also ask you, what are the odds this is just a coincidence?

Knowing that the continuous expansion of mathematical combinations are as endless as time itself makes it very difficult to believe the connections of all these numbers could be accidental. So, not only is this proof that Christ's number of 13,333 is the correct marker for the calendar; but also, most if not all that has been brought to light to this point must also be correct.

And from all that I have learned, I now personally believe the following Biblical verse is one that has been completely misinterpreted for almost two thousand years. For it's in John 2:19 that Jesus had just driven the moneychangers from the Temple courtyard when the high priests demanded He should show them a sign and prove to them He was sent by God to do such a thing. But Jesus refused and instead, stated, "destroy this Temple and I will raise it up again in three days." Christ's disciples believed He had spoken metaphorically in referring to the fact that He had conquered death and had arose again on the third day. But 2 Peter 3:8 states "but beloved be not ignorant of this one thing, that *one day is with the Lord as a thousand years, and a thousand years as one day.*" And this one verse makes it clear that Christ was not referring to His death and resurrection, but was in fact stating He would literally return within three days and rebuild the Temple. Therefore, two thousand years plus Christ's age of thirty-three when He last departed the earth equals the year 2033, which will be the dawning of the third day in the realm of God.

Now that the marker has been found and more revelations can be brought to light, it's time to view an updated version of the calendar.

The Life of Christ on the Pyramid Calendar

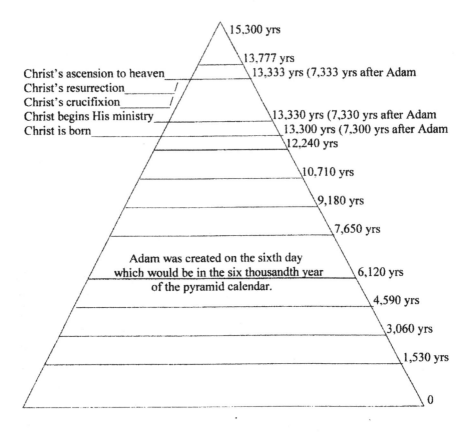

15,300 yrs

13,777 yrs

13,333 yrs (7,333 yrs after Adam

Christ's ascension to heaven
Christ's resurrection
Christ's crucifixion
Christ begins His ministry
Christ is born

13,330 yrs (7,330 yrs after Adam

13,300 yrs (7,300 yrs after Adam

12,240 yrs

10,710 yrs

9,180 yrs

7,650 yrs

Adam was created on the sixth day
which would be in the six thousandth year
of the pyramid calendar.

6,120 yrs

4,590 yrs

3,060 yrs

1,530 yrs

0

First, note that Christ was born in the *13,300th* year of the calendar. From knowing that the Exodus took place *1,300* years prior to His birth we now know that the Exodus took place in the *12,000th* year on the pyramid calendar. This struck me as simply amazing in recalling from that earlier chapter in which it was revealed how the number *12* mathematically connects God and Christ together as one.

Next, once again note that Christ was born in the *13,300th* year of the calendar and then *thirty* years later He began His ministry in it's *13,330th* year. And then *three* years afterwards, His crucifixion, resurrection and ascension occurred in the *13,333rd* year of the calendar. Now notice how it's the very same numbers which denote all the major events of Christ's life on the pyramid calendar that are the very same Biblical numbers that denote all the major events of His life on earth. He was born *1,300* years after the Exodus, He was the *13th* apostle, He began His ministry at the age of *thirty*; He was crucified, resurrected, and ascended in the *33rd* year of His life; and He arose on the *third* day. It's here that one has to concede at just how astonishing it is that the Biblical numbers which signify the major events of Christ's life on earth are the very same numbers marking those same events on the pyramid calendar.

But that's not all; once again, note that Adam was created in the 6,000th year and that Christ was born *7,300* years after Adam; and that Christ began His ministry *7,330* years after Adam. And still yet, that He was crucified, resurrected, and ascended *7,333* years after the creation of Adam. I was immediately fascinated with the fact that from the creation of Adam till the birth of Christ was 7,300 years; and, that the pyramid calendar had also revealed the number *73* marking every major event of Christ's life on earth. Now there were two sets of numbers that had followed the life of Christ on the pyramid calendar in which the number 13 marked His birth and life on earth. And yet, the number 73 had done the very same thing in the number of years between the creation of Adam until His birth. But, moreover, I also knew from my previous writing that the number of years between the Israelites reclaiming Jerusalem in 1967 and the return of Christ in 2040 will be *seventy-three* years. Now to see seventy-three on the calendar also marking Christ's life on earth is to say in the very least, a jaw dropping moment for me. So, there is no question in my mind about whether or not this number is associated with Christ; no, the question in my mind is, just what does it mean? So could there be a secret to the number 73 and its association to Christ that's just waiting to be revealed?

Chapter 12

73 and 37 . . . What a Pair!

It was learned in my previous book that the date of the 2012 prophecy consisted of numbers that are mirrors of one another, such as twelve and twenty-one, thirty-six, and sixty-three. And it was also learned that God's wrath will begin in the year 20**37**; and, its mirror image, **73,** is the number of years between 1967 when the Israelites reclaimed Jerusalem, and the return of Christ in 2040.

Since it appears the number 73 will mark the return of Christ in the future; and, since the birth of Christ is marked on the pyramid calendar with the number 73, then this number is a direct reflection on Christ Himself. Therefore the question that must now be asked is, why is this number connected to Christ; just what does it signify?

At one point in my last book I placed a man on the supposed mercy seat of the Ark and then made what I thought was my own humble attempt to speak as I felt God Himself would have spoken in that particular situation. And in one line from that scene I stated *"let him who is wise see the future by seeing the past."* At the time I assumed that line came from me, but now I'm not so sure because by the time I had finished that book it had became apparent that the more I had researched and dug into the Bible's Old Testament books of the past the more I could see into the Biblical future. And, when I started this book I was only doing what I knew I had been led to do. I did not have one earthly clue that I was going to find all that has been revealed to this point. And yet, here I am again, having come full circle and about to have the future revealed to me by looking into the past.

The first clue to Christ's relationship to the number 73 lies in that it will be 73 years from the moment the Jews reclaimed Jerusalem 1967 until His return in 2040. And in doing so it becomes apparent that 73 has something to do with His return to earth. And when looking again at the pyramid calendar, one can see that 73 also marked the birth of Christ.

Since 73 marks the major events of Christ's life within the pyramid calendar maybe it's time to take another hard look at the pyramid itself. Language is spoken in many different dialects and this includes Math. So the question is, what mathematical dialect is God speaking in the design of the pyramid? It's obvious that its outer shape is in the form of a triangle; therefore, the pyramid is geometrical.

And since the pyramid's design is a form of geometry; and all major events of Christ's life on earth have been found within that geometrical design marked with the number 73; is it possible that this number itself is also of a geometrical design?

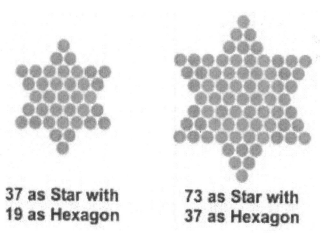

**37 as Star with
19 as Hexagon**   **73 as Star with
37 as Hexagon**

And the answer to that question is yes; 73 is a star number, and not only that, but its mirror image 37 is also a star number. And when Christ was born what was it that hovered in the sky over His manger, but the "Star of Bethlehem."

So, it has now been discovered that the outer geometrical design of the Great Pyramid forms a Biblical calendar. And found within that calendar was the number 73 which forms the geometrical design of a star. And this geometrical star number marks the birth, the ministry, the crucifixion, the resurrection and the ascension of Christ on that geometrical calendar. And this directly coincides with the Bible's claim that there was a strange bright star in the sky upon the birth of Christ. And this is enough to make one wonder just what are the odds that all of this is a coincidence? But, the calendar's number 73 marks Christ entering the world at a time when He called for brotherly love, peace and salvation for mankind. And seventy-three years from the moment the Israelites reclaimed Jerusalem, He will once again return peacefully to the world with the righteous in Him.

So what about 73's mirror image thirty-seven? Just what does it represent concerning Christ? The only place it's seen is within those seven years of the tribulation in 2037 which is to be the year for the wrath of God. But according to Revelation, it will not be God who will do the actual pouring out of that wrath. But, it will be Christ who will be the One to open the seals that set loose the four horsemen of the apocalypse. The only time in His earthly life that Christ displayed an emotion of anger was when the moneychangers had defiled the sanctity of His Father's Holy Temple. So, if the Antichrist occupies that Holy spot in 2036, mankind will have once again defiled His Father's Holy Temple. Therefore, Christ will once again display His anger toward mankind by unleashing His Father's wrath upon the world. Revelation also states that it will be Christ who will defeat Satan at the battle of Armageddon and cleanse the world of evil. So 73's mirror image, 37, represents an angry wrathful side of Christ.

And yet, there is even more evidence that these two star numbers are symbolic of and represent the return of Christ. For in the book of Mathew, Christ describes to His disciples how He will appear when He returns; Mathew 24:27 "For as the lightning cometh out of the east, and shineth even unto the west; so shall also the coming of the Son of man be." This verse reveals that Christ's return will be announced by the appearance of a huge bright light, and what else could that be but a star? And again, although it's an angel that shows John all that is revealed to him in Revelation, at the end Christ Himself speaks directly to John. Revelation 22: 16 states "I, Jesus, have sent mine angel to testify unto you these things in the churches; I am the root of David; and, the bright and morning star."

These verses along with the math of the pyramid calendar reveal that Christ's return will be announced in the same manner as when He first arrived, by the appearance of a star. Therefore both the star number 73, and its mirror image 37, proclaim the arrival of Christ.

And because these two numbers can change positions to become each other, then not only are they mirrors of one another, but they are also inverted numbers which means they face in opposite directions. And when looking closely at the picture of the stars above one can see two pyramids fused together facing in opposite directions, which answers the question about that emblem on the Pope's ring. For it's correct that it's the emblem of a star. But . . . it's not the seal of Solomon, nor is it the star of David. Math is the universal language of God and numbers don't lie, and the pyramid calendar makes it plain that *this is the star of Christ.*

And as if knowing all of this is not astounding enough within its own right, in chapter six of *"Lee Strobel's"* book *"The Case For A Creator"* Mr. Strobel interviews "Dr. Robin Collins," who holds doctorate degrees in physics, mathematics, and philosophy, and is a researcher, writer, and an associate professor of philosophy at Messiah college. During this interview Dr. Collins refers to "Fred Hoyle," an English Astronomer, who back in the 1950s stated "there is a precise process by which carbon and oxygen are produced in a certain ratio inside stars, if you tinker with the resonance states of carbon, you won't get the materials you need for building life." Then Dr. Collins noted that recent studies by the physicist, "Heinz Oberhummer," and his colleagues show that just a one percent change in the strong nuclear force would have a thirty—to a thousand fold impact on the production of oxygen and carbon in stars. "And since stars provide the carbon and oxygen needed for life on planets, if you throw that off balance, conditions in the universe would be much less optimal for the existence of life."

And in now knowing that a star's perfect balance of carbon and oxygen must exist in order for life itself to begin to exist, one must ask just how odd is it that it was a star that signified the beginning of the life of Christ?

Chapter 13

They Have Eyes Yet Still do not See

Since it's now obvious this star was not seen in the skies over Israel during the time of David or Solomon, but instead during the life of Christ, it leaves one to ask; why would those of the Jewish faith invent legends that attributed David and or, Solomon credit for the star that actually, denotes the birth and life of Christ? And the answer to that question is that those Jews of the Orthodox faith from the time of Christ to this very day still do not believe that Jesus was their Messiah. In fact, they are even now still waiting for God to send them their promised messiah. And knowing this only further substantiates that the Bible and the math of the pyramid calendar are correct, and that this celestial event actually happened. For if the nation of Israel had not witnessed a strange star in the sky upon the birth of Christ, then they would not have felt the need to invent legends and myths to assign the semblance of that event to someone whom they did believe in, like their former kings, David and Solomon.

In my studies of the Bible I have noticed subtle ironic undertones in many of its stories; therefore, I have come to believe that God must be a big fan of irony. And from knowing what I've just learned I can't help but chuckle. For how ironic is it that the nation of Israel would adopt the star that marked the birth and the life of Christ as their official emblem, proudly displaying it all over their country and on their flag while at the same time denying that Christ is their Messiah.

But knowing all of this is also revealing in other ways. In Mathew 24:16-18 Christ tells His disciples what the Israelites should do once the Antichrist arrives: 16: "Then let them which be in Judea flee into the mountains;" 17: "Let him which is on the housetop not come down to take anything out of his house;" 18: "Neither let him which is in the field return back to take his clothes." Up until this very moment I had thought these verses meant the Israelites would be driven from their land by the Antichrist upon his arrival. But, now I know what Christ was really telling His disciples was that for those who would know Him at that future time, should at that moment flee Jerusalem. Because those of the Jewish faith will have just embraced a deceiver as their God sent Messiah. And this leads one to wonder why they will believe the Antichrist when they have refused to believe Christ? And again, the answer to that question lies in referring back to chapter eleven and John 2:19 in which Jesus refused to show the hierarchy of the temple a sign that He was sent from God. They had demanded a miracle, and when none was given to them they did not believe Christ was their Messiah; after all, if He was truly sent by God then surely He should prove it and perform a miracle, shouldn't He?

The books of Mathew and Luke make virtually the same statement in explaining why Jesus refused to give them their miracle. Luke 11:29 states "This is an evil generation; they seek a sign; and there shall be no sign given it." So in other words, because they had once again stopped obeying God's laws and no longer sought Him in His Spirit and in His truth, but instead sought after themselves, seeking their own truth, they were blind and could not see that Christ was their God sent Messiah. And this fact is self evident, for if they had continued to obey God's laws, seeking His truth, they would've known who Christ was. Therefore, they would not have needed a miracle. But, more important is the fact that even to this very day those of the Jewish Orthodox Church still refuse to accept Christ as their Messiah because they will only accept one that will give them their miracle. And this is why they will embrace the Antichrist because he will give them that miracle.

2nd Thessalonians 2:11-12 states "And for this cause God shall send them a strong delusion, that they should believe a lie. 12: That they all might be damned who believe not the truth, but had pleasure in unrighteousness."

Revelation chapter 19:20 states "And the beast was taken, and with him the false prophet that wrought miracles before him, with which he deceived them that had received the mark of the beast, and them that worshipped his image."

And it's here that one can see another supreme case of God's mysterious irony within His works. For it was the hierarchy of the Jewish church that did not recognize Christ and had Him crucified. And it will be these same people who will still not know Him, and therefore will believe a deceitful miracle, and then announce to the world they have found their Messiah while embracing an imposter.

From the moment God restored to Israel it's ancient and holy city in 1967 Israel was given seventy years to come back to God and obey His laws, seeking His truth, and recognize His Son as their only true Messiah.

And what will happen if Israel fails to do so? Then as I have previously stated, *"Let those who are wise see Israel's future by seeing Israel's failure to do so in the past."*

But it's not just Israel who will face the wrath of God in 2037 because Revelation makes it plain this false prophet will perform such marvels and wonders that he will deceive the very elect of many nations. And therefore the leaders of those nations who follow him will lead their people down a deceitful dead end path, filled with dreadful death and destruction.

Psalm 9:17 states "The wicked shall be turned into hell, and the nations that forget God."

So I ask you who are reading this book, just how important is it for America to remember their God and His Son as their Savior? Just how vital is it that the American people elect leaders who know and fear God and will put His laws back on their government buildings, and prayer back in their schools?

But for the moment, perhaps the even more important questions to ask are; who will be this false prophet; how is it that he will be able to perform such great miracles; and where will he come from?

Chapter 14

Hell and the Bottomless Pit

There are many people in today's world including Christians who no longer believe hell is an actual place. They've managed to convince themselves that no matter what type of a life they have lived, a loving God would never condemn them to such an atrocious eternity. But, what does the word of God say concerning this now presumed fantasy world called Hell?

When referring to the Bible and all the verses that are found within it that makes references to Hell, it becomes apparent this place really does exist. It's spoken of a total of fifty-four times throughout scripture. And in the New Testament chapter of Luke it's Christ Himself who tells the story of a rich man who never bothered to aid a beggar named Lazarus, and upon his death he wakes up in hell and sees Lazarus lying peacefully within the bosom of Abraham, to which he begs Abraham to let Lazarus dip his finger in water and let it drip on his tongue to cool his torment from the flame for just a second.

But, Abraham refused and gave two reasons as to why he would not honor the rich man's request. First; the rich man was reminded of his ungodliness treatment of Lazarus while receiving good things in his earthly life, and Lazarus being a Godly man received evil things from him. Secondly, Abraham states there is a great gulf that separates them which prevents the rich man in hell from coming to where he and Lazarus are. And also prevents him and Lazarus from going to where he is.

And this is not the only time Christ speaks of a place of fiery torment, for He also states in the book of Mathew what will happen when He pours out His Father's wrath. 13: 41-42 states "The Son of man shall send forth His angels, and gather out of His kingdom all things that offend, and them which do iniquity." "And shall cast them into a furnace of fire: there shall be wailing and gnashing of teeth." And again in Mathew 25:41 Jesus states "Then shall He say also to them on the left hand, depart from Me, ye cursed, into everlasting fire, prepared for the devil and his angels."

Not only do these verses confirm that hell actually exists, but they also resonate with Revelation's description of what will happen to those left behind following the rapture in which chapter 14:10-11 states "The same shall drink of the wine of the wrath of God which is poured out without mixture into the cup of his indignation; and he shall be tormented with fire and brimstone in the presence of the holy angels and in the presence of the Lamb." "And the smoke of their torment ascendeth up for ever and ever; and they have no rest day or night."

So, if one is going to accept the Holy Bible as the true word of God, then one hasn't any choice but to accept the fact that hell does indeed exist and is a real place. Since it has been confirmed there is a physical place called hell, then the next question to ask is; where is this place of fiery and eternal torment located?

Referring back to Christ's story of the rich man Abraham stated there was a great gulf between them, and since it can be assumed Abraham and Lazarus are in Heaven, then this great gulf must be what separates Heaven from Hell. So, just what is it that divides these two places? The definition of gulf is a deep ravine, chasm, or *abyss*, and herein lies a major clue. For in the New Testament there are references made to a place called *the deep, and the bottomless pit*, also known as the *abyss*. And the definition of an abyss is a **deep** bottomless chasm.

In the book of Luke, Jesus approached a man who was possessed of demons, and when Jesus commanded these evil spirits to come out of the man they begged Jesus not to send them into the **deep**. So is it possible those demons were asking not to be sent into the great gulf that separates Heaven from Hell? Ask many Biblical scholars if they think Hell, the abyss, and the bottomless pit are one and the same place and they will probably say yes. But is this Biblically correct?

One could certainly get the notion that Hell is the bottomless pit from reading certain verses from the book of Revelation. Revelation

9:1-2, 11 states "And the fifth angel sounded; and I saw a star fall from heaven unto the earth; and to him was given the key to the bottomless pit. 2," "And he opened the bottomless pit; and there arose a smoke out of the pit as the smoke of a great furnace; and the sun and the air were darkened by the reason of the smoke of the pit." 11, "And they had a king over them, which is the angel of the bottomless pit, whose name in the Hebrew tongue is Abaddon, but in the Greek tongue hath his name Apollyon."

From these verses it could easily be concluded that the bottomless pit with it's smoke and the evil angel that dwells within it must be a reference to Satan and His home of Hell. And there are many who believe that's exactly what these verses are describing.

But actually, nothing could be farther from the truth because other verses in Revelation make it clear that Hell and the bottomless pit are two distinctly separate places. Revelation 19:20 states "And the beast was taken, and with him the false prophet that wrought miracles before him, with which he deceived them that had received the mark of the beast, and them that worshipped his image. *These both* were cast alive into the lake of fire burning with brimstone."

So the false prophet and the beast of the bottomless pit will be cast into the lake of fire in Hell. But there will be three evil entities working to deceive mankind during the tribulation. And while this verse makes it clear what will happen to the false prophet and the beast, it makes no mention of Satan, so what does God do with him?

Revelation 20:1-3 states "And I saw an angel come down from heaven, having the key of the bottomless pit, and a great chain in his hand." "And he laid hold on the dragon, that old serpent, which is the Devil, and Satan, and bound him a thousand years." "And cast him into the bottomless pit."

These verses reveal that God literally makes the beast and Satan trade places. The beast is now in Hell and Satan is bound with a chain and then locked inside of the bottomless pit. Therefore, Hell and the bottomless pit are two different and separate entities.

Now that it's been determined hell does exists, and that hell and the bottomless pit are two different places, the question now becomes; where are they located?

Most Biblical scholars who believe in Hell claim it exists beneath our very feet within the core of the earth. And there are verses that can be found in scripture that support this claim. Paul, in the book of

Ephesians 4: 9 states "Now that He ascended what is it but that He also descended first into the lower parts of the earth." And in Mathew 12:40 Jesus Himself stated "For as Jonas was three days and nights in the whale's belly; so shall the Son of man be three days and three nights in the heart of the earth." And there's also that verse by John of Patmos in which he states in Revelation 13:11 "And I beheld another beast coming up out of the earth; and he had two horns like a lamb, and he spake as a dragon."

These verses reveal that the scholars are correct and that Hell is actually located somewhere beneath the surface of the earth. And in knowing this it becomes apparent that the great gulf spoken of by Abraham is what divides both Hell and the Earth from Heaven.

No doubt many would say the great gulf which separates the Earth and Hell from Heaven is simply the distance to somewhere on the other side of the universe hundreds of millions of light-years away. But, Abraham didn't say there was a great distance, or expanse, or even space, he stated there was *a great gulf* between them. And in Revelation John speaks of an evil angel who ascends from out of *a bottomless pit*. And the definitions of a gulf and a bottomless pit are very similar. A gulf is a deep ravine, chasm, or abyss, and the synonyms used to describe a bottomless pit are chasm and abyss. So could it be possible that Abraham and John were referring to the same place? And if they were, then where would this great gulf which may also be known as the bottomless pit be located?

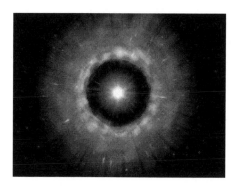

Chapter 15

Black Holes In Space

In 2002 NASA's Chandra's X-ray Observatory revealed what scientist's previously suspected was located at the center of our Milky Way Galaxy, which was a large black hole. Since this discovery scientists have learned much concerning black holes in space. It's been discovered that they can be found at the center of most all the galaxies within our universe, and it seems that black holes may also play a role in the creation of the stars within their galaxies. And scientists also believe that it's possible that black holes themselves may have started out as stars.

Smaller stars live for several million years while the larger ones burn out much sooner, living for only a few million years. Stars are powered by nuclear fusion and go through radical changes toward the end of their life expanding into massive red giants. Once the smaller stars become red giants their cores collapse into what's referred to as white dwarfs with their outer edges spewing out planetary nebula. These nebula contain the basic building blocks for life such as carbon, nitrogen, oxygen, and calcium.

But the larger stars go supernova, which is a process whereby they explode, expelling most of their mass in a burst of radiation so intense that a shock wave is sent throughout the surrounding stellar medium, and the light from this explosion is often times brighter than an entire galaxy. The core of the star then collapses into what is called a neutron star or black hole. And this black hole is created as a result of the constant intense gravitational pull on what's left of the burning dense core of what was once the star.

Authors note:

If you happen to be one who read my last book then I apologize for reentering familiar territory. But, just as the planets are in the geometrical shape of a circle and orbit each other in circles, it seems at least for now as though God is doing the same with me. And in searching for only His truth and no one else's I must go where He leads, even if it's in a circle.

There's an article in the June 2011 issue of Discover Magazine in which "Steve Nadis" interviewed Astrophysicist "Andrew Hamilton." Mr. Hamilton has made the study of black holes in space one of his specialties and is considered to be a leading authority on this subject. During this interview Mr. Hamilton made the following statement in his description of how he perceives a black hole. "Relativity is confusing enough for conventional objects: It is far stranger for a black hole because such an object does not merely dent space time; it creates a discontinuity, a bottomless pit in the middle of an otherwise smooth fabric."

So, is it a mere coincidence that in the book of Revelation John refers to a beast that ascends from out of a bottomless pit and now almost two thousand years later an authority on black holes in space compares them to a bottomless pit? So, is it possible that the great gulf that separates the realm of the earth from the realm of Heaven, lies within that huge black hole at the center of our Milky Way Galaxy?

I am sure scientists would say the odds of anything ascending from out of a black hole are next to impossible simply because of the number of obstacles that would have to be overcome, the greatest of those being that the tremendous pull of gravity within the hole itself would certainly shred anything that entered it into less than microscopic sized particles. So, a beast arising from out of a black hole in space can be ruled out simply because of the gravity enigma can't it? Or can it?

It was previously made obvious that the ancient Egyptians could not have built the pyramids by themselves. As you might recall, the stone coffer was sawed out from a block of solid red granite which required bronze saws eight to nine feet in length using teeth set with sapphires. And then it was hollowed out with a fixed point drill that used hard jeweled bits with a drilling force of two tons. But, just as important is the fact that the weight of some of those blocks used in the construction of the pyramids weighed as much as seventy tons, and this makes it impossible to accept the notion they were moved into place by nothing more than ancient manual labor. Therefore, it leads to question just how were those massive sized stones moved into position in the creation of the pyramids?

From all that's been learned concerning the Great Pyramid it leaves little doubt that its design came from none other than God Himself. Therefore, it only makes sense that those involved in the building of the pyramid were not bound by the universal law of gravity. Therefore those huge blocks were merely levitated into place by removing the force of gravity from around them. And since they had the capability to displace gravity from around blocks of stone weighing as much as seventy tons, then it's also conceivable that they were able to move the force of gravity aside as they traveled through a black hole.

And if it were to be possible that one could actually travel through a black hole then where would it take them? To another location within our own universe? Or even possibly to an alternate universe? Or would its function be similar to that of a time machine, taking you forward into the future, or backward into the past?

In the same interview in Discover magazine Mr. Hamilton talks of how he uses computer models to better understand the strange interior of a black hole. He then states at one point he plugged a spinning black hole into one of these models and began dropping imaginary particles into the hole to see what would happen. And he found that when a particle falls into a black hole and approaches the inner horizon it's diverted into one of two narrowly focused, laser like beams. If the particle entered in the direction opposite that of the black hole's rotation it would join an ingoing beam that has positive energy and move it forward in time. But if the particle entered in the same direction as the black hole's spin, it joined an out going beam that has negative energy and moved the particle backward in time.

Mr. Hamilton also proposed a new analogy to describe what happens when something approaches a black hole's event horizon, likening it to a waterfall crashing into an abyss. A fish can swim near the edge and safely slip away unless it gets too close, in which case it will be dragged over the precipice no matter how hard it resists. Similarly, any object or even any kind of energy is swept across the event horizon by a waterfall of space that is constantly cascading into the black hole. Mr. Hamilton also described *a black hole as "a place where space is falling faster than light."* ("No object can move through space faster than light, but there is no restriction on how quickly space itself can move.")

So if Mr. Hamilton's analogy were to be correct, and my analogy were to also be correct, in which one could move the force of gravity from their immediate surroundings, then depending on from what direction they entered a spinning black hole they could be propelled either forward or backwards in time traveling faster than the speed of light.

Revelation 13:18 states "Here is wisdom. Let him who hath understanding count the number of *the beast*; for it *is* the number of *a man*; and *his number is six hundred threescore and six."*

Revelation 17:8 states *"The beast* thou sawest was, and is not; *shall ascend out of the bottomless pit."*

So is it possible that someone is about to travel backwards in time from the future in an attempt to deceive the world into believing he is the Son of God by performing false miracles through his advanced knowledge and technology from the future?

But moreover, is it possible to find a connection to the bottomless pit and the number 666?

The Ancient Mayan's knew over one thousand years in advance that on 12/21/2012 the Earth's sun would begin to come into alignment with that giant black hole at the center of our galaxy. And this date was so important to them that they built a huge stone calendar to reinsure that the world would not forget the importance of it. But oddly enough, at the same time they failed to reveal to the world as to what they expected to happen, if anything, on this date. Scientists have recently learned that there is a mirror within the event horizon of a black hole, therefore a black hole projects a mirror image of anything that falls into it while concealing what really happens on the other side of it's event horizon. And from learning to see spirits within the numbers of dates, I saw the number 12 mirroring the number 21 three times within the date of 12/21/2012, or (**12212012**). And as you may remember from chapter six the three twelve's added up to **36**, and when 36 was seen as spirits and added together they became 3+6 = 9. And when the mirrors of the three twelve's, the three twenty-ones were added together they added up to **63**, which is a mirror image of **36**, and when seeing these two numbers as spirits they also added up to 6+3= 9. So, what about the three twelve's and their mirrors, the three twenty-ones? What happens these numbers are added together three times, and then their totals seen as spirits and added together?

12+21=33, and 33 seen as spirits and added together is 3+3 = **6**.
12+21=33, and 33 seen as spirits and added together is 3+3 = **6**.
12+21=33, and 33 seen as spirits and added together is 3+3 = **6**.

And let's not forget that these numbers of 12, 21, 36, and 63 are numbers that are mirrors of each other; and also, that the black hole at the center of our galaxy has a mirror within it's event horizon, and that the date of 12/21/2012's numbers themselves are mirrors of each other, and that it's also on this date in which the earth's sun will align with that black hole at the center of our galaxy.

In the book of Revelation John makes it clear he is foretelling of an event that will take place just prior to the return of Christ, therefore John is foretelling of a future event. But the question that is not answered by John is; is this event predestined to happen, or is it a warning of what might happen. And if it is a warning, then what is required of mankind to avoid it?

Chapter 16

Exposing the Miracles of the Beast

In the thirteenth chapter of Revelation, John sees a beast rise up from the sea having seven heads with ten horns and ten crowns. Then one of the beast's seven heads receives a deadly wound that is healed which causes the world to marvel after the beast. Then in chapter seventeen an angel appears and tells John that the beast he saw was really a man, and that the sea he arose out of is really the bottomless pit, and that the seven heads on the beast represent seven kings, in which five have fallen, the sixth is currently in power with one more to come. And that the beast (aka the man) will be the eighth king; and, that he was also one of the previous seven.

When comparing what John had witnessed when he saw the beast in chapter thirteen to that of the angel telling John that the beast is actually a man in chapter seventeen, the pieces of this puzzle come together revealing a great miracle to be performed by the beast. In knowing that he will be a man who will receive a deadly wound that will be healed reveals why the world will believe he is the risen Christ, and therefore cause people to wonder whose names are not written in the book of life slain from the foundation of the world.

Remember, five kings will have fallen with the sixth currently in power, with one to come for a short time, *and the beast himself will be the eighth, and he will also have been one of the previous seven.* This in essence states that he will rise to power as the sixth king, then disappear for a short time, then reappear as the eighth. Now let's recall that John had seen seven heads on the beast and that one of those heads received a deadly wound but was healed, and that it represents one of the previous seven kings.

And what was the greatest earthly miracle performed by Christ, but that He died the physical death and rose again on the third day. So, the Antichrist knows the surest way to deceive the world into believing he is the risen Christ is to make a name for himself by rising to the position of a king, then he will allow himself to be killed, only to come back to life.

But the question is, how will he accomplish this feat? One possibility may lie in that he may be from the future. If he has traveled backward in time and then allows himself to be killed, is he also dead in the future? Or would he merely return to where he is in the future, and therefore able to return again? Scientists and fiction writers alike have a field day over the many possible outcomes of this theoretical paradox. And since as far as it's known, it's not currently possible to perform this feat of time travel; then there's no way of knowing of what would really happen.

But since it's obvious that those who built the pyramids were not bound by the law of gravity; and since John stated a man will ascend from out of a bottomless pit, and since scientists refer to that black hole at the center of our galaxy as a bottomless pit; and since computer models reveal that black holes could possibly propel objects either forward or backward in time faster than the speed of light; it then becomes a theory that must be seriously considered as possible.

The next event in Revelation that concerns the beast occurs when a second beast appears from out of the earth having two horns like a lamb speaking as a dragon making fire come down from Heaven and performing all the miracles and wonders as the first beast. This second beast then calls for the masses to worship and honor the first beast whose deadly wound was healed by building an image in his likeness. Then once the image is made the second beast gives life to the image so that it can both speak and kill those who do not worship the first beast or his image. Then the second beast forces everyone to receive a mark of the image of the first beast either in their forehead or in their right hand. John then states that here is wisdom; let him who has understanding count the number of the beast for it is the number of a man and his number is six-hundred threescore and six.

But, could it be possible that this second beast and the image that is built in honor of the first beast are forms of an advanced technology? One possible clue is found in Revelation 13:14 which states, "And he deceives them that dwell on the earth by the means of those miracles which he had power to do in the sight of the first beast." This verse reveals a possible and serious weakness of this second beast in that it must always be within sight of the first beast for it to have its power.

So, could this second beast be a form of an advanced holographic image, or even possibly a clone that is actually being controlled by the first beast? And let's no longer envision the image to be built in the likeness of the first beast to be akin to that of a statue made of stone, but rather let's see it for what it will truly be which will be a form of an advanced technology whose purpose will be to mark and track the location of all mankind. Revelation 13:15-17 states the second beast will give life to the image of the first beast so that it can both speak and kill those who do not worship the first beast or it's image, and all the people must have the mark of the beast before they will be allowed to buy, sell or trade.

These verses reveal that the sole purpose for the creation of this image of the first beast will be to gain control over all the people on earth by implanting tracking devices in them in order to monitor their movements. But, what if this implanted mark of the beast is more than just a device that sends information to the image revealing where you are at all times; what if this advanced technology is also able to read your thoughts and if you allow the wrong thought to enter your mind you could die instantly. How hellishly suffocating and frightening would that be, not even being allowed to have control of you own mind, and always living in fear of instant death just from thinking the wrong thought?

When these verses are seen from this perspective it really drives home yet another verse in which John states, "For who can be like unto the beast; who can make war with him?" But moreover, it also reveals how easy it would be for a single person who with the support of a small select group of followers who have exclusive unregulated access to an advanced technology to take control of and rule the world.

Now just imagine someone in the not too distant future who has access to such an advanced technology with the same determination to rule the world as that of Adolph Hitler. And speaking of Hitler, just where did the technological age that we currently find ourselves caught up in originate, but from Hitler and Nazi Germany? And what was the first thing they did when they got hold of it, but to use it to their advantage in an attempt to conquer and rule the world.

Chapter 17

Exposing the Image of the Beast

Two verses in Revelation have been studied by countless Biblical scholars and researchers for almost two thousand years because of their intriguing, yet very vague clues about the identity of the beast, in which John states,

> *"And he had power to give life unto the image of the beast. And no man might buy or sell except he has the mark, or the name of the beast or the number of his name." "Here is wisdom, let him who hath understanding count the number of the beast, for it is the number of a man, and his number is six hundred three score and six."*

The reason for these being the most scrutinized verses in the Holy Bible is because John is speaking of the future end of the world. Therefore it's believed if the beast could be identified it would reveal when the end of this current world is to happen in the future. And throughout the ages, it's also been believed that the key to solving this riddle would be by attaching the number 666 to the name of a man. And from the way those verses are worded it would appear to be correct to do so. But, two thousand years of taking that approach to those verses has not revealed anything of any significance.

As a result from continuous research in the writing of both books I had constantly read those verses over and again. But not so much as an attempt to know and unravel the mystery of the number 666, but rather, to better understand how the beast, who will also be a man, will attempt to become nine evil spirits in the year 2036. Therefore I noticed within these verses in which the world is to build an image of the first beast, that two key words stood out in relation to the beast. And while knowing if solved, they would not directly identify the man, I knew they would identify the beast, which in turn might also identify the man.

So, I began to take a hard look as to a possible hidden meaning within those two words which might reveal the identify of the beast, which were *the **mark** and the **image** of the beast*. And since both these words are a direct reference to the beast, I also felt if the mystery was solved to one, it would in turn, reveal the hidden meaning of the other.

So I asked myself; what would be the definition of the word *mark* in terms of it's relation to an *image*? "And the words that came to mind were; symbol, sign, insignia, logo, and trademark. This revealed that the image of the beast would be a symbolic logo, and or, a trademark of the false prophet. Now, I was beginning to feel as though I was on the right track because this also answered how the beast could at the same time, also be a man. He will adopt and be known by a symbolic image which will become his trademark.

And from now knowing this, I instinctively knew that image was going to be one that would be exceedingly blasphemous toward God. Therefore, I began a Biblical search for clues that might reveal the image that the Antichrist would use for his symbolic trademark.

But, after numerous hours of searching and coming up empty I was told that what I sought would be found in the same place where both books had begun, at Mount Sinai.

Therefore, I began reading the book of Exodus searching for an image that would be blasphemous toward God, while totally unaware that the answer that I sought would literally lie at the foot of that mountain.

For it was at Sinai where Moses spent forty days and nights receiving the Ten Commandments from God. And the very first two Commandments that were carved into those stone tablets are as follows.

1. Thou shalt have no other gods before Me.
2. Thou shalt not make unto thee any graven image, or any likeness of any thing that is in Heaven above, or that is in the earth beneath,

or that is in the water under the earth. Thou shalt not bow down thyself to them, nor serve them: for I the Lord thy God am a jealous God, visiting the iniquity of the fathers upon the children unto the third and fourth generation of them that hate Me.

It's within these two commandments in which God makes it clear that He is a jealous God who will not tolerate the worshipping of graven images and false gods. But, He also goes onto state that His very reason for casting the plagues on Egypt was to punish the children of the third and fourth generations because they no longer worshipped Him, but instead worshipped graven images and false idols.

This lead to a search of Egypt's most highly worshipped pagan god. And as a result it was discovered that the Egyptians worshipped many mythological gods that were both part human and part animal. But there was one animal the Egyptians worshipped that was not part human, and was held in the highest of esteem as the supreme deity above all their gods.

And upon his return from the mountain Moses found that the Israelites had already turned away from God and had melted their gold and fashioned it into the likeness of the very same animal that the Egyptians had heralded as their god above all gods, which was that of a young bull.

Exodus goes onto state that as a result of that blasphemous act God became so incensed with anger He told Moses He was going to destroy all of them and make Moses a great nation. In which Moses had to remind God of His covenant with Abraham, and that He had already promised him it would be his seed that would spring forth His nation. So in other words, God had became so angry over their worshipping of that golden calf that God Himself almost sinned. And having connected this incident to John's statement in Revelation concerning the image and the mark of the beast I was now convinced the identity of the image that the Antichrist will use as his official trademark had been revealed, which is that it will be the image of a bull.

And in recalling that the Antichrist will rule many nations in his attempt to conquer the world; the next thought that came to mind was, if the world is close to the end of time, then those nations should already be joining together. Therefore, would it be possible to find such a group of nations who had adopted as their trademark the symbolic image of a bull?

Chapter 18

The Rise and Fall of the Fourth Kingdom

In the seventeenth chapter of Revelation the angel shows John a woman dressed in scarlet and purple sitting on a scarlet beast who has seven heads with ten horns wearing ten crowns. Then the angel proceeds to tell John the beast is actually a man who will ascend from out of the bottomless pit; and the woman is the great whore Babylon. Next, the angel explains that the seven heads stood for seven kings and seven mountains in which Babylon is located, and that within its midst there are many nations, multitudes, and tongues. The ten horns wearing ten crowns represent ten kings who receive power one hour with the Antichrist, and because they hate Babylon they will use their power to attack and destroy it; and, upon completion of this feat they then return their power as kings back over to the Antichrist.

These verses reveal that the Antichrist will be crowned as a king by this unknown city of Babylon, then he will allow himself to be killed, only to return and once again be crowned as a king. But, upon his return he will be working behind the scenes to have ten nations attack and destroy Babylon. Therefore the question becomes why will he destroy the very city in which he rises to power? One possible aspect for his destruction of Babylon is that it's not Jerusalem, which is where he will attempt to rule the world from the temple built in his honor on Mount Moriah. Therefore, it's likely there will be those in Babylon who will know things about him that he doesn't want the world to know so he will have it destroyed before making his move to Jerusalem in order to cover his tracks.

But, more important for the moment is that John and the angel have given valuable clues to the location and the identity of Babylon. First, it will be a great city that's readily recognized by its symbolic colors of scarlet and purple. Second, it sits in the same geographical location in which there are seven mountains. Third, it's surrounded by many nations of various people speaking different languages. And yet, another valuable clue is mentioned in chapter eighteen in which it states a huge stone will be cast into the sea and Babylon will be found no more. This reveals that Babylon is located next to a large body of water; and, that perhaps it's final demise will be from the result of a tidal wave caused by either an asteroid or a meteor strike upon the ocean.

And still another clue lies in knowing that the Antichrist will have control over a mighty kingdom consisting of many nations in which most of them will be working together in an attempt to achieve the same goal, which is that together they will rule the world.

From having so much revealed to me concerning the future by studying the past, I once again turned to the Old Testament in an attempt to find this kingdom, and as a result I came upon the book of Daniel in which he tells King Nebuchadnezzar there would be four world kingdoms before the fifth and final kingdom of Christ would be established. Daniel identifies these kingdoms by their metals in which he sates the first will be a kingdom of gold, the second of silver, the third of brass, and the fourth of iron mixed with clay. And Daniel also sates this fourth kingdom will be divided, but will eventually attempt to reunite to its former power; and, that the clay mixed with the iron means it will not succeed. And most historians agree that the kingdoms Daniel was referring to are as follows: First, the gold was ancient Babylon, which ruled from 605 until 539 BC; the second kingdom of silver was that of the Medo-Persian Empire, which ruled from 539 until 311 BC; the third of silver was the Greek Empire, which ruled from 311 until 168 BC. And the fourth kingdom that was divided and will attempt to rise again is that of the Roman Empire which held power from 168 BC until AD 476.

So, let's go back and check the clues that John received from the angel and see if it's possible they apply to the city of Rome. One clue was that Babylon was located within seven mountains. There are seven hills east of the River Tiber in Rome which are also commonly referred to as the seven mountains of Rome. Another clue stated Babylon would be buried under water and found no more. Rome is located approximately twenty miles from the coast of the Tyrrhenian Sea, which is an arm of the Mediterranean. The next clue was that the woman was dressed in scarlet and purple which means these are the symbolic colors of Babylon. During its rule ancient Rome had the largest army in the world, which was known by it's soldiers who wore uniforms of red. And yet, the final clue was that Babylon sat in the midst of many nations, peoples, and tongues. Rome is located in Italy; and, Italy has many nations of people from various origins speaking different languages all around it.

Since it appears Rome fits the criterion for being the great city of Babylon, and it's located within the nation of Italy, then the next question became, does Italy belong to a united group of nations whose desire it is to control and eventually rule the world?

The Treaty of Rome, previously signed by six countries, formed what was known as the *"European Economic Community"* on January the 1st 1958. These countries consisted of Belgium, France, Italy, Luxembourg, the Netherlands, and West Germany. Their stated purpose for unification was to be a deterrent to being invaded by foreign entities and to promote democracy. By 2007 their membership had grew to twenty-seven countries and they had changed their name to "The European Union," but are commonly referred to as the EU. In 2009 the "Lisbon Treaty" went into effect which took the governing policies away from the EU's voters and gave that power solely to the elite of the EU's Socialist controlled Parliament. In its beginning, the EU lured other nations to join them simply through it's appeal of economic stability and security. But now that its membership has become so large the EU plays a major role in Europe's financial markets which in turn directly affects the economic stability of all the nations of Europe. As a result, independent nations with struggling economies are now literally being forced to join the EU and concede their rights and their freedoms over to the polices of the EU's Socialist controlled Parliament just to avoid their own economic collapse. There is now growing concern that the EU will continue in this manner until it has moved itself into a position to force the governments of all nations around the world to surrender to its controlling policies in return for economic stability, and that it's the EU's long term goal to establish themselves as leaders of a one world government with control of a one world financial market based on the Euro making it the only monetary denomination on earth.

And since you are reading this book then consider yourself forewarned that on the very day America is forced to join the EU because of its own failed economy that document which guaranteed you your freedom and your rights known as the Constitution will have just become null and void.

And if the Eu is successful in its attempt to rule the world, then there will only be one accepted form of religious worship, and it's easy to see which sect is poised to assume this future position simply by recalling where the EU signed up its first six members, which was at the "Treaty of Rome." And just walking distance from Rome lies the Vatican, which happens to be headquarters for the Roman Catholic Church, which is also the world's largest with over one billion members. Now let's recall that the angel stated Babylon could be identified by its colors of scarlet and purple, and that both Rome's and the Catholic Church's prominent symbolic colors are scarlet and purple. And yet another clue was that Babylon was surrounded by many nations consisting of people of various origins speaking in different tongues. The EU consists of nations filled with people from various cultures that speak numerous different languages. But, perhaps the most significant clue that the Antichrist will rise to power from within Rome and the European Union is that the EU's symbolic trademark is that of the image of the God Zeus, who in Greek mythology assumed the form of a bull in order to seduce the mythological lady Europa to mount him, at which time he kidnapped and raped her.

**Statue of Zeus kidnapping Europa in front of
the European Union's Council building.**

And since the ancient Greeks blended much of their mythology to that of the Egyptians, it's believed by many that Zeus assumed the form of Egypt's most highly worshipped bull known as Apis which is the same bull the Israelites were worshipping when Moses returned from Mount Sinai.

But this statue is not the only place in which they proudly display the image of Zeus kidnapping Europa. It's also the official image used on their stamps, coins, and even their magazines. And yet, there is even more evidence that Babylon, spoken of by the angel, is in fact the city of Rome and the Vatican. For there is a story in the book of Genesis in which a tyrant named Nimrod brought all the people together in a land called Babel and convinced them that God had no right to succumb mankind to a lower level than that of the upper heavens. And as an act of defiance they began building a tower in an attempt to reach those upper heavens and force God to reveal Himself to them. But God caused them to speak in different tongues which left them confused and therefore they were unable to finish it. The EU's new parliament building was completed in

1996 and its main tower closely resembles "Pieter Brueghel the Elders" 1563s painting of "The Tower of Babel."

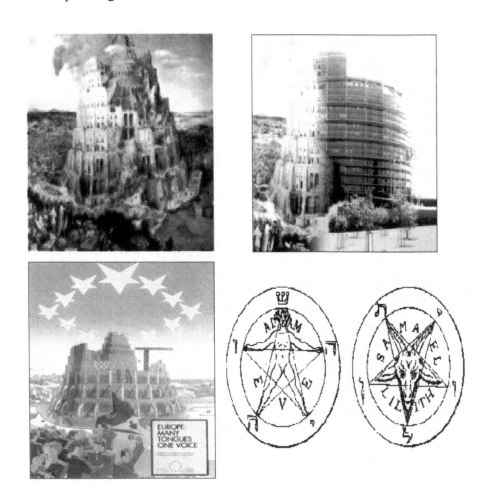

And a poster put out by the EU offers even more evidence that the tower of their parliament building was meant to resemble that of the Tower of Babel. Note that the stars above the poster's tower are upside down. A star right side up represents a hexagram, but a star in the inverted position represents a pentagram which is the sign for Satan. The lower right hand corner of the poster proudly proclaims "Europe: Many Tongues One Voice." And also, the European Union's Parliament has 679 seats, but only 678 members with one seat left vacant as though it's reserved for someone who is to appear at some time in the future. The seat that remains empty for now is seat number 666.

If a man from the future is soon to ascend from that bottomless pit at the center of our galaxy with the intention of deceiving the world into believing that he is the risen Christ, then he will have to select and adopt a church as his own. And once again, where did the EU get its roots, and who is at the center of all this, but Rome and the Roman Catholic Church? And furthermore, once he allows himself to be killed and returns, having performed this miracle, the Jewish Orthodox Church will then also believe he is their God sent Messiah and begin building a temple for him on Mount Moriah in Jerusalem. And it's here that this may be God's greatest work of irony since the creation of mankind. For it was the nations of Rome and Israel who did not recognize Christ and together crucified Him. And now it appears it's going to be these very same two, who because they still won't know Him, will together embrace the Antichrist, while believing and attempting to convince the world they have found Christ.

The angel also stated the seven heads on the beast not only represented seven mountains, but that they also stood for seven kings in which five are fallen, the sixth will be currently in power, with a seventh ruling for a short time, and the beast will be the eighth; and, that even he will have been one of the previous seven. This reveals the beast will be both the sixth and the eighth king of Babylon in knowing that he will allow himself to be killed; and, then upon his return he will replace the seventh king who will have just recently taken his place. The angel also states that ten *nations* will attack and destroy the *city* of Babylon, but at the same time it's Babylon who will crown the Antichrist as a king. So how is it that it will be a city and not a nation that will have the power to crown him as a king? Is it possible that the angel is really referring to the kings of a church who's known for bestowing a crown to its leaders? And moreover, the heart of the Roman Catholic Church is located in what is known the world over as Vatican *City*.

In the sixth chapter of Revelation John sees the four horsemen of the apocalypse in which the first one is riding a white horse carrying a bow, and then a crown is given to him as he goes forth conquering and to conquer. This could easily be considered symbolic of a man donned in a white robe and wearing the crown of the Pope. And if this were to be correct, then the question becomes, how do we count and identify the previous five Popes in order to know when the Antichrist will arrive to become the sixth?

From knowing all that has been revealed from both my previous writing and now this one, I instinctively knew the starting point for the counting of those kings, aka Popes, would have had to begin in 1967. And the Pope in that year was Paul the VI, who reigned until 1978. He was followed by John Paul I, who died under mysterious circumstances after having held the title for only thirty-three days. He was followed by John Paul the Great, who was the Pope until 2005, at which time he was followed by Benedict XVI, who at the writing of this book, is the fourth and current Pope since 1967. So if it's correct that the angel was referring to Popes rather than kings, then there will be one more after Benedict, and the Pope who follows him will be the sixth, therefore he should be the Antichrist making his first appearance, claiming his reserved seat number of 666 in the European Parliament.

Authors note: Christ had a major following of many Jewish people who believed and accepted Him as their God sent Messiah. It was when He entered Jerusalem that the priests of the Temple saw Him as nothing more than a threat to their own high positions within the church. So in order to secure their places within that church, they lied about Christ and had Him crucified. And while it's most likely that there are hundreds of millions of people of the Catholic faith who know Christ as their Savior, I must, at the same time, in my search for the truth, also say that there is something in the makings within the Vatican and the European Union that within its very nature amounts to nothing less than pure evil.

Chapter 19

The New Tower of Babel?

In knowing that the EU's Parliament seat number 666 remains empty, and therefore reserved, makes one wonder, just who are they waiting for? Where will he come from? And when is he due to arrive? Is it possible that the EU, in a sense, has rebuilt the Tower of Babel right under the world's nose?

In 1998, "The European Organization for Nuclear Research" began construction on what is now the largest particle accelerator in the world known as the "Large Hadron Collider," or more commonly referred to as the LHC. It consists of a seventeen mile circular tunnel over 300 feet beneath the earth's surface and is located on the Franco-Swiss border next to Lake Geneva Switzerland. It was completed, making its first successful run in 2008. This collider strips electrons from hydrogen atoms, creating protons, and then these protons are split by sending them in opposing directions around the circular tunnel and smashing them into each other at near the speed of light.

At top speed, the opposing beams make 11,245 trips around the seventeen mile collider every second, which in turn causes 600 million explosions of protons every second. The LHC states that in doing this they will gain an insight and better understand how the universe was created, saying that on the subatomic level, this process may mimic what happened to within mere seconds, following the big bang. Another thing they are hoping to find is the Higgs boson, which is a hypothetical elementary particle that is predicted to exist by the standard model. But it has also been mentioned that this process may also produce momentary miniscule black holes similar to the one at the center of our galaxy. And still yet, another possible result from smashing these protons into each other is that it may create an opening within the earth's dimension revealing an alternate dimension. And, at one point it was stated by scientists that if this were to happen it may even reveal the very face of God. Which was what Nimrod and his followers were trying to do when they built the Tower of Babel; they wanted to see and confront God.

Yet, God has never physically revealed Himself to mankind. He spoke to Moses through a burning bush, and later, through the Ark of the Covenant. Therefore, any attempt of any type to force Him to physically reveal Himself would achieve nothing less than being blasphemous toward the very will of God.

The Large Hadron Collider's function is to violently force subatomic particles into each other which are the very essence of what makes up this universe. Yet if we are to believe in a God, and that He created this universe, then it should be obvious that when subatomic particles must be forced to smash into each other at the speed of light resulting in violent explosions that this goes against the very nature by which God created this universe.

When the LHC made its first successful run in 2008 it was at an output of 7 trillion electron volts. The latest update on 02-14-2012 was that they intend to ramp up that output by 14 percent to 8 trillion electron volts by late November of this year. It will then be shut down for twenty months and revamp to 14 trillion electron volts when it starts up again in either late 2014 or early 2015. And as the voltage increases so will the intensity of the proton explosions, which in turn will cause those miniscule black holes to become that much larger.

So, is it a mere coincidence that on 12/21/2012 our sun will come into alignment with that mirrored black hole at the center of our galaxy; and, that the mirrored numbers in 12/21/2012 total to 666, or that the EU's parliament has an empty seat number of 666? And is it also a coincidence that within the heart of the European Union lies the world's largest machine which costs over 6 billion dollars to build? And that it's this machine's sole purpose to split the very particles which make up the essence of this universe by violently smashing them into each other in attempts to create a hole and see on the other side of creation? And is it a coincidence that it will soon have 14 trillion electron volts running through it with a huge mirror in the form of a lake close by which could become a large conductor of that electricity? In his new found knowledge of technology has mankind become so zealous and impatient to know his true origin that he has forgotten the most basic law of nature? Has not even one of these scientists bothered to consider Newton's law that for every action there must and will be an opposite and equal reaction? And is this mankind's latest way of making the same mistake that he has made in his past? Are not these scientists, in their blind lust to find the creator, forsaking the most basic law that makes up the very nature and the very will of our God?

Many Biblical scholars state that the beast rising up from out of the sea is not a literal term, but rather the word sea is a metaphor meaning he will rise to power from out of the masses. And they get this interpretation because they assimilate it to the angel's statement to John that the great whore that sat upon many waters was actually symbolic of many people, tongues, and nations. But the angel did not state to John that the sea in which he saw the beast rise up from represented anything other than what he had actually seen. Therefore, John saw the beast literally rising up from out of a large body of water. And if he had viewed this water from close range he may have assumed it was the sea when it could've just as easily have been a large lake. And once these scientists succeed in going against the very nature of creation and turn Lake Geneva into a black hole similar to the one at the center of our galaxy, God has already spoken through His prophets, and has forewarned the world what will happen once this pit has been opened.

2nd Thessalonians 2:11 states "And for this cause God shall send them a strong delusion, that they should believe a lie. That they all might be damned."

Revelation 9:1-2 "And he opened the bottomless pit; and there arose a great smoke from out of the pit, as the smoke of a great furnace; and the sun and the air were darkened by reason of the smoke of the pit." Revelation 9: 3-6 "And there came out of the smoke locusts upon the earth; and unto them was given power, as the scorpions of the earth have power, and it was commanded of them that they should not hurt the earth, but only those men who have not the seal of God in their foreheads. And they should be tormented five months; and their torment was that of a scorpion when he stings a man. And in those days shall men seek death, and shall not find it for death shall flee from them.

Revelation 9: 11 "And they had a king over them, which is the angel of the bottomless pit, whose name in the Hebrew tongue is Abaddon, but in the Greek hath his name Apollyon."

Revelation 13: 1 "And I stood upon the sand of the sea, and saw a beast rise up out of the sea, having seven heads and ten crowns, and upon his heads were the name of blasphemy."

Revelation 17: 18 "The beast thou sawest shall ascend out of the bottomless pit

Revelation 13:18 "The number of the beast is the number of a man; and his number is six hundred three score and six."

Isaiah 24:17-22 "Fear, and the pit, and the snare are upon thee, O inhabitant of the earth. 18—"He who flees from fear of the noise shall fall into the pit; and he that cometh up from out of the pit shall be taken in the snare: for the windows on high are open, and the foundations of the earth do shake." 19—"The earth is utterly broken down, the earth is clean dissolved, the earth is moved exceedingly." 20—"The earth shall reel to and fro like a drunkard, and shall be removed like a cottage; and the transgression thereof shall be heavy upon it; and it shall fall, and not rise again." 21—"And in that day the Lord shall punish the ones on high, and the kings of the earth." 22—"And they shall be gathered as prisoners into the pit, and shall be shut up in the prison."

And here lies yet another case of irony at its finest. For how is it that these scientists can be so intelligent, yet be so blind from their own lust to find the creator that they haven't the first clue that what they are searching for is the God of the Holy Bible? Someone should inform these people that Einstein's announcement that the universe had been created did not verify that there was a creator; no, Einstein's acknowledgement of a creator only verified what had already been told to the world thousands of years earlier from the word of God. And if these people would bother to take the time to read His book then they would know that the only way God will allow mankind to seek Him is through the acceptance of His Son as the Savior; and also, that there are laws by which man must abide. Yet, these people have no fear of God, and dare not to break just His Commandments, but break a law that goes against His very nature, while at the same time, attempting to force Him against His will to reveal Himself to mankind.

So, I would like to quote to these scientists from an old saying that was very popular where I was employed for almost thirty years which is, "be very careful in creating that hole for someone; you just may be creating it for yourselves."

Chapter 20

Coincidences to Huge too Ignore

The Bible states the Antichrist will be an imitator of Christ. Jesus began His ministry at the age of *thirty*, and at *thirty-three* He was crucified, resurrected and ascended back to His realm of heaven. In the writing of both books I've made it perfectly clear I am convinced the year 2033 will be the dawning of the third day in the realm of God, which in turn will be the beginning of the tribulation here on earth. So, if my timeline is correct then it only makes sense that the Antichrist will be known around the world by coming to power in the year 2030. Therefore, three years later he will enter Jerusalem in 2033. And Revelation states he will occupy Jerusalem for three and one half years, which puts him entering the new Temple in the year 2036.

Both the Bible and the pyramid calendar say the birth of Christ was announced by the arrival of a star. And 2nd Thessalonians states the Antichrist will be sent to the world by none other than God Himself because the world has once again turned away from worshipping Him and obeying His laws. Since God sent a star to the world announcing the arrival of His Son as the Savior, then would He also send a sign to the world as a warning that His Son will soon pour out His wrath?

In 2004 an asteroid was discovered at the Kitt Peak National Observatory by Roy A. Tucker, David J. Tholen, and Fabrizio Bernardi. It was later learned that this object, which is 690 by 1,080 feet in diameter, would make a close rendezvous with earth, coming within 18,300 miles of impact on Friday April the 13th in the year 2029. This will be so close that not only will the asteroid be visible with the naked eye, but its spin state will also be affected by the tidal forces of the earth's gravity field. Tucker and Tholen are fans of the TV series Stargate SG-1 and named the asteroid after one of its villains who goes by the name of the Greek god "Apophis" who is also known in Egyptian mythology as "Apep" who is the serpent god of eternal darkness and chaos, and also referred to as the "un creator."

And while it now appears Apophis will miss the earth in 2029 it still runs a risk of entering a narrow corridor of space known as the *keyhole*, in which the earth's gravity could change its orbit and put it on a collision course with earth seven years later in 2036.

Since these dates line up with the seven years of the tribulation in which the asteroid will pass by the earth just prior to the Antichrist entering Jerusalem, and then possibly make impact at the time of him entering the new Temple makes it a coincidence to huge too ignore. And when you add in the fact that it has been named after an Egyptian god of destruction, then not only does it become a strange coincidence, but it also takes on the eerie aurora of a Biblical prophecy.

Revelation 18:21 states "And a mighty angel took up a stone like a great millstone, and cast it into the sea, saying, thus with violence shall that great city Babylon be thrown down, and found no more at all." In the eighth chapter of Revelation John observes two stars fall from Heaven, but in the eighteenth chapter he states he sees a mighty angel pick up a great stone, not a star, and that it will be cast into the sea to destroy Babylon; and, what else could this great stone be but an asteroid?

But this also fed my curiosity as I began to wonder if it were possible to distinguish any of the other entities that would descend from the sky in Revelation. Thus, I began taking a closer look at what John was saying as he attempted to describe these falling objects.

And the first incident that takes place in which it appears something falls from the heavens begins when an angel casts a golden censer into the earth. This causes a great earthquake followed by hail and fire mingled with blood to fall from the sky. And it would seem as though these things are falling from the upper realm of the earth's atmosphere, but in the next verse John sees a great mountain burning with fire as if it were cast into the sea. And this makes it clear that John was actually seeing fiery stones covered with lava from a volcanic eruption. Next, note that John did not say a mountain fell from the heavens, but that it was cast into the sea. So the question then became; is there a volcano somewhere upon the earth that could be cast into the sea as the result of an earthquake?

The Cumbi Viegja volcano located on the island of La Palma in the Canary Islands erupted in 1949 which was followed by an earthquake that opened a fissure 1.6 miles long on the eastern side of the volcano's summit. As a result the western side of the volcano slid six and one half feet downwards and three and one half feet westward toward the Atlantic Ocean. The western half of the volcano has a mass of 1,500,000,000 metric tons. If it were to suddenly slide into the ocean it would generate an initial tidal wave of over 3,000 feet at the island, and an estimated height of between 40 and 100 feet when it reached the North American Continent approximately eight hours later. This tidal wave would have the potential of killing hundreds of millions of people by literally wiping out cities along the Atlantic seaboard from Boston Massachusetts to Miami Florida, and all the way to Havana Cuba. Scientists studying this volcano have concluded it would take several eruptions before it would have the potential of falling into the sea, and even then, it's likely only parts of it would collapse and not the whole land mass at once. But these scientists may be making a huge error in studying only the volcano's likely eruptions. The reason for the volcano's initial slide was not from its eruption, but from the ensuing earthquake; and, it seems these scientists have not taken this likely possibility into account. John states there will be a great earthquake just prior to the mountain being cast into the sea. Therefore a real possibility exists that the earthquake itself will cause a tsunami which in turn will only add to the height of the tidal wave caused by the volcano's slide into the ocean. The potential result of this being that the wave would be much larger than its current estimated height of 40 to 100 feet when it hits the Atlantic seaboard. And John also gives an insight to just how catastrophic this event will be in that one third of the ocean will turn blood red, and one third of all the ships and marine life in the sea will be destroyed.

Many people in today's world refuse to believe a loving God would cause such catastrophic events as those described in Revelation. But God, for whatever His reason, has chosen not to reveal Himself and speak personally to the world. From the very beginning He has only revealed Himself in Spirit, in the minds of His chosen prophets, speaking to mankind by sending messages through them. And at times those messages were warnings of an impending wrath because man had fallen away from and forgotten his God. He revealed to only one man on earth an advanced warning that He was about to destroy mankind. And, when Noah began building the Ark and attempting to warn the people of the coming flood they refused to believe God would do such a thing; and so, they laughed and made fun of Noah right up until the rains began. When He first spoke to Moses it was through a burning bush. He then spoke through Moses to Ramses to set His people free. And later, He spoke to Moses through the Ark, and through him to the Israelites. It was God who destroyed mankind with the flood. It was also God who used nature to cast ten plagues on Egypt. It was God who opened up the earth and had it to swallow those who opposed Moses in the desert. And again, it was God who drowned Ramses' mighty army in the Red Sea. And it was also God who rained hell fire down from the sky on Sodom and Gomorrah. So, just as God has done in the past, He has already spoken through John of Patmos and warned the world what will happen when mankind has once again forgotten Him. Which is that He will speak His anger in the same way that He has spoken it in the past, which will be through catastrophic natural disasters.

And if and when this happens, because mankind will have fallen so far away from the truth of God; and, because scientists will be so blind in their lust to find the creator, mankind will not recognize and acknowledge that these natural disasters are being caused by God. But at the same time, they will not hesitate to curse His name because of them. Revelation 16:9 states "And men were scorched with great heat, and blasphemed the name of God, which hath power over these plagues; and they repented not to give Him glory."

Chapter 21

An Unheeded Warning Becomes Destiny

From its beginning to its end, the Bible is constantly conveying the message that somewhere in his past man turned away from the righteousness of God and fell into sin. The result being that mankind was corrupted for all future generations causing man to have to die the physical death. But, because God loves His creation of mankind so much, He offered man salvation through Christ in whom he could be forgiven of his sins and once again become perfected through His righteousness and receive eternal life.

And God's final phase for instituting that plan began the moment of that covenant at Mount Sinai, in which His most precious gift to His chosen people were His Commandments. And as long as the Israelites honored and obeyed these laws they were seeking the truth of God; for His truth lies within His laws. But once they had defeated all their foes and felt secure in their land they felt they no longer needed God; so, they turned away from Him and His Commandments. He then sent the Israelites a warning form the prophet Jeremiah to turn back to Him or have their kingdom taken from them. Yet, their response was not to turn back; but instead, they took that most sacred artifact which held those Commandments from its Holy place in the Temple and hid it underground. The end result of this was that their kingdom was destroyed by the Babylonians and those of the blood line of David were taken captive and reduced to being slaves in Babylon for seventy years.

God then gave them another chance to come back to Him and they were allowed to return to Jerusalem and rebuild the Temple a second time.

But by the time the Israelites had been sent their promised Messiah they had once again stopped obeying His laws and seeking Him in His truth. Therefore, they did not recognize Christ as the Savior of the world and crucified Him. And although they had committed this horrible act, God still gave them seventy years to turn back to Him and see Christ for who He really was. And when they failed to do so, God allowed their second Temple to be burned to the ground in what is said to be one of the most ghastly wars in history. It's stated by the historian "Flavius Josephus" who was present during this war, that not only did the Roman army destroy and burn Jerusalem beyond recognition, but that the Temple and the Mount on which it stood was so seething hot from the flames that all the gold and silver inside melted and ran down into the cracks between its stone walls; and, that the Romans in their greed to retrieve it turned over every stone. And this literally fulfilled Christ's prophecy in which He had told His disciples that not one stone would be left on top of the other. Josephus also stated that everywhere one looked there were dead bodies stacked up like cords of wood, and that in the aftermath to keep from starving to death the women ate their young. And from knowing all this it would seem as though Jerusalem had become nothing less than a burning Hell. Which is exactly what God had previously told David would happen to the nations that forgot Him.

Psalm 9:17 states *"The wicked shall be turned into hell, and the nations that forget God."*

And knowing this was the fate of the nation of Israel for not obeying God and failing to recognize Christ as their Messiah, and in knowing that these are God's own chosen people, do the nations around the world today really believe they too can turn away from God, forsaking His Son, yet not become blind, unable recognize a false Christ, and that the same fate of Israel's past awaits them in their near future?

It's obvious that John's vision in Revelation is both a warning and a prophecy. First, it's a warning to all nations not to forsake the laws of God and His Son as the Savior of mankind. In fact the main topic spoken throughout the Bible is that it's constantly driving home the point for mankind to stop his repetitive insanity of turning away from God; and instead, remember that only by obeying His laws can humanity remain under His righteous protection and be truly blessed. But at the same time John's vision is also a prophecy of what's going to happen to those who refuse to accept Christ as their Messiah, and through Him seek the Father in His Spirit and in His truth. Which is that they are soon about to be turned into hell.

But the previously quoted verse also makes it clear that the tribulation can be avoided simply because it states that the beast, who is really a man, will not come here of his own accord, but rather, that he will be sent here by none other than God Almighty Himself. And in the very same chapter of Second Thessalonians it also states that the Antichrist cannot come to deceive the world unless there is first a falling away of the world from God. And yet again, there's also that verse from the apostle John which states in chapter 3:17 "For God sent not His Son into the world to condemn the world; but, that the world through Him might be saved." So, if all the nations around the world would accept Christ as their savior and through Him seek the truth of God there would be no tribulation. But since it doesn't currently appear as though that's going to happen, then the question still remains, just who is this beast?

It's in chapter seventeen of Revelation in which the angel states that the beast is actually a man, and that he ascends from out of the bottomless pit. So who is this man that's soon to be sent here by God through the great gulf to deceive the world?

Isaiah 14: 12-16 states "How art thou fallen from heaven, O Lucifer, son of the morning! How art thou cut down to the ground, which didst weaken the nations:" 13—"For thou hast said in thine heart, I will ascend into the heavens, I will exalt my throne above the stars of God: *I will sit also upon the mount of the congregation*, in the sides of the north:" 14—"I will ascend above the heights of the clouds; I will be like the most High." 15—"Yet thou shall be brought down to hell, **to the sides of the pit.**" 16—"They that see thee shall narrowly look upon thee, and consider thee saying, *Is this the **man** that made the world to tremble, that did shake the kingdoms:*"

So why would God cast Satan down to the earth among mankind when He could just as easily cast Him somewhere on the other side of the universe? Although it's obvious this question has been answered throughout this book many times over, I want to answer it yet again, for a final time.

"*And for this cause God shall send them a strong delusion, that they shall believe a lie. That they all might be damned.*" And what is God's cause for doing this? Because the world will have forsaken Him, His laws, and His Son as the Savior of mankind. And the end result form this will be that the world's destiny will be right back to where it was before God offered His plan of Salvation. Which is that it will once again become a lost and dying world without hope. So, the final question really isn't why would He do this, oh no; the final question is, . . . why wouldn't He?

Authors note:

It should now be apparent that we, as individuals, as nations, and as a world, have only one of two real choices to make while we are here on this planet. We either choose Christ as our Savior, accepting His Spirit into our soul, and not just receive eternal life, but receive it more abundantly. Or we choose to live solely in the flesh, dying a physical death, and awake to an eternal hell. There are no other choices. And if you think there are, then no one can deceive you, not the Antichrist nor even Satan, because you have already deceived yourself.

Summation

When reading the Bible it becomes apparent that even if mankind were to be alone in this universe there still must exist another realm that man cannot see from which this world is being observed. And through His Holy Word and His Son, God created a path that gave a lost and dying world hope for salvation and eternal life. All that has been required of mankind is to simply follow it. But, it's obvious from these revelations that not only is mankind refusing to take that path, but that this generation through its abuse of modern technology, will soon blaspheme God in more drastic ways than ever before possible in the history of the known world. And once that black hole is opened, breaking not just the law of His nature; but also, attempting to force Him to reveal Himself, He will send the world a deceiver. And the world will then worship a false god and desecrate that holy ground in Jerusalem. But once His wrath is being poured out by an angry Son, mankind will come into remembrance of his true God.

And if America as a nation is to avoid that wrath, then its people better remember and come back to God by obeying His laws and accepting Christ as their savior. Its citizens should not just demand that its government's leaders put prayer back in its schools and God's Commandments back on the walls of its institutions, but to also abide by those laws.

And America should never, for any reason, become a member of the European Union. For any nation associated with the EU will no longer be in control of its own destiny; but, a mere pawn caught up in a blasphemous game of fools totally unaware that what they really seek is the wrath of God. And from now knowing what the LHC is attempting, and that it goes against the very nature and the very will of God, America should demand the Large Hadron Collider be turned off and dismantled until the year 2041; because, by then Christ will have returned and therefore it won't be needed. And any nation who opposes America in this stand should be told to go to Hell. For it has been made clear that Hell will soon be the new home for any and all nations that support this endeavor.

It's my prayer that those who read this book will see and recognize the truth of it. For I am an ordinary man who has spent most of my past thirty years working two full time jobs. Therefore, how is it that I suddenly know all that has been revealed within these pages, other than, since it couldn't have come from me, that it had to have came through me from somewhere else?

And while much has been brought to light and many questions answered within this book, there are still many that has yet to be. Questions such as; why were there *three* crucified the day Jesus paid the price for the sins of all mankind? Why was it that when He arose again that it was on the *third* day? Why do Egypt's *three* main pyramids align with the *three* main stars of the belt of Orion? And why does the shaft in the king's chamber of the Great Pyramid point to Orion? And what was God's reason for putting His mark on that spot in Egypt? Could it be the that the position of the pyramids are marking the direction and the distance to somewhere? Although it's not God's desire to personally reveal Himself to the world, could it be that He has shown us where He lives? If one could ride on a beam of light leaving from the shaft of the king's chamber in the Great Pyramid and headed straight for Orion, and then continue past it for a total of 15,300 years, would it take them to the city limits of Heaven? Although for now that question will remain unanswered there is one thing that those who are alive in the Spirit will soon experience which is, *"behold; I show you a mystery, we shall not all sleep; but, we shall all be changed, in a moment, in the twinkling of an eye,"* and then who knows, in that moment, it just may be revealed to us where He lives.

87081778R00060

Made in the USA
Middletown, DE
01 September 2018